Frontispiece:
A view of the central area of the Cahokia site taken from a low oblique angle viewed from the southwest. Monks Mound is in the background and in the foreground are Fox Mound (Number 60) on the right and Roundtop (Number 57) on the left.

EXPLORATIONS INTO CAHOKIA ARCHAEOLOGY

Edited by
Melvin L. Fowler

ILLINOIS ARCHAEOLOGICAL SURVEY, INC.
Bulletin No. 7
University of Illinois
Urbana

To promote a greater understanding of the
prehistory and early history of the State
of Illinois.

1973
Revised Edition

PREFACE

Last year was the 40th anniversary of Warren King Moorehead's publication on the Cahokia site. He had spent several years in working at Cahokia excavating many of the mounds. His publication is today the only adequate statement on the Cahokia site available. Commemorating the work at Cahokia by Moorehead, we are presenting this volume as the most complete statement on the Cahokia site since Moorehead's day. The present volume is the result of many years of work at the Cahokia site and the work of many people. In this regard it differs from Moorehead's publication in that it presents a diversity of viewpoints and interpretations.

Specifically this volume is the outgrowth of a symposium on Cahokia that was presented at the 33rd Annual Meeting of the Society for American Archaeology held in Sante Fe, New Mexico May 9th, 10th, and 11th, 1968. Three papers appearing in this volume were not part of that symposium. One, by Miss Harriet Smith, reports on the excavations at Mound 55 of the Cahokia group undertaken by her in 1941. This paper was presented at an earlier symposium held at the meeting of the Central States Anthropological Society in St. Louis in 1965. Another paper is by Warren Wittry and is reprinted here by courtesy of the Cranbrook Institute of Science. The third paper, not a part of the symposium, is on corn remains at Cahokia and related sites by Hugh Cutler and Leonard Blake.

These papers published in this bulletin cover a wide range of subjects including general descriptions of the Cahokia site, questions of chronology, and reports of specific excavations that have not been previously discussed in the literature. One of these papers, that by James Porter, dealing with the Mitchell site, presents data on a group of mounds that are outside of the main Cahokia zone and also a general theory regarding economic aspects of the Cahokia community.

All of the papers of this volume are but preliminary reports of research that is going on at the present time and in that sense should not be considered as the final and definitive statements on the Cahokia site. Even so, those of us participating in the various symposia, conducting current research at Cahokia, and concerned about this problem felt it important to present a statement at this time for several reasons.

One reason is that there is a tremendous amount of data accumulating on this site that is not known to the scholarly profession and to the general public. It is important to present a summary of this data so that colleagues and interested persons might be informed. A major obligation of the archaeologist is that he present his material since archaeology is part of our public heritage. Another reason, and perhaps the most important, is that without doubt Cahokia is, at the same time, the largest and most important archaeological site in North America and also the least understood and most neglected. It is hoped that in presenting this information an understanding of the fact of the immensity and complexity of Cahokia will be partially understood by others and that perhaps such a volume as this can serve as a stimulus towards correcting the neglect and misunderstanding of the Cahokia site.

Over the years many people have been concerned with Cahokia and have tried to summarize the extant knowledge, to understand the site, and to see if the errors of our concern and understanding about this site could be remedied. These people have been many and some of them are discussed in the first paper in this volume. One of these persons was the late Dr. Paul F. Titterington of St. Louis, Missouri, who over the years has given a great deal of his attention to the problems of Cahokia and at one time even financed a publication bringing together the information available to him at that time. If this present volume were dedicated to any single person, it would be to Dr. Titterington in gratitude for his work and efforts since he stands as a symbol for those many other people who have attempted to see that something was done about Cahokia. Another outstanding person in the Midwest who, over the years, attempted to do something about Cahokia and pled with state officials and other people to preserve the site was Dr. John Francis Snyder. Snyder, a medical doctor, was born in a house built upon one of the mounds at the Lunsford-Pulcher site at the south end of the American Bottom and spent much of his childhood in the area of Cahokia mounds. Over the years as an adult, he also devoted himself to archaeological research and did some of the truly pioneering work in the Illinois area. Our concern with Cahokia and the reasons for publishing this material at this time are probably best summarized by Snyder's statement regarding archaeological work in Illinois in general:

> But some light may yet be shed upon the dark page of their ethnography and migrations by persistent, systematic and intelligent study of the broad and inviting archaeological field our state represents. With some highly creditable exceptions, antiquarian research in Illinois has heretofore been conducted principally by curiosity mongers and mercenary vandals for selfish gain only. It demands, and should receive, before it is too late, the earnest attention of active, scholarly workers in the interest of science.

(Snyder, 1911: 302)

M.L.F.

TABLE OF CONTENTS

PREFACE
   by Melvin L. Fowler v

THE CAHOKIA SITE
   by Melvin L. Fowler 1

MONKS AND OTHER MISSISSIPPIAN MOUNDS
   by Nelson A. Reed 31

THE AMERICAN WOODHENGE
   by Warren L. Wittry 43

THE MURDOCK MOUND: CAHOKIA SITE
   by Harriet M. Smith........................... 49

A CAHOKIA PALISADE SEQUENCE
   by James Anderson 89

SOME CERAMIC PERIODS AND THEIR IMPLICATIONS AT CAHOKIA
   by Patricia J. O'Brien........................ 100

CORN FROM CAHOKIA SITES
   by Hugh C. Cutler and Leonard W. Blake 122

THE MITCHELL SITE AND PREHISTORIC EXCHANGE SYSTEMS AT
CAHOKIA: AD 1000±300
   by James Warren Porter 137

BIBLIOGRAPHY 165

LIST OF FIGURES

Page

Frontispiece   View of the central area of the Cahokia site from a low
oblique angle

Fig. 1   Map of the American Bottom area showing the locations of
sites discussed in the volume 2

Fig. 2   Topographic map of the Cahokia Mounds archaeological site from
the USGS quadrangle sheet 3

Fig. 3   Two recent oblique photographic views of Monks Mound 4

Fig. 4   Segment of the Collot map showing the location of St. Louis and
the Lunsford-Pulcher site 6

Fig. 5   Drawing of the Cahokia Mounds area published in 1841 9

Fig. 6   Drawing of Monks Mound published in 1844 9

Fig. 7   Drawing of Monks Mound published by McAdams 10

Fig. 8   Central portion of Cahokia as mapped by A.J.R. Patrick 11

Fig. 9   Aerial photograph of the Monks Mound area taken by 1st
Lieutenant Goddard in 1921 13

Fig. 10   Aerial mosaic of the Monks Mound area made by Col. Dache
Reeves in 1933 14

Fig. 11   Oblique aerial views of ridge-top mounds 16

Fig. 12   View of Powell Mound from the south 17

Fig. 13   Central section of the Cahokia site map made by the University
of Wisconsin-Milwaukee 18

Fig. 14   Central section of the Cahokia site showing alignments of mounds
to Monks Mound and Mound 72 20

Fig. 15   The post pit at the eastern end of Mound 72 21

Fig. 16   Two views of the excavation of the Mound 72 post pit 22

Fig. 17   The primary mound surface at the eastern end of Mound 72 23

Fig. 18   The central burial in the Mound 72 primary mound 24

Fig. 19   A group of six burials near the central burial in the Mound 72
primary mound 25

Fig. 20   One of the arrowhead caches buried with the individuals in
Fig. 19 26

Fig. 21   The Patrick map of Monks Mound made in 1876 32

Fig. 22   Topographic map of Monks Mound 34

Fig. 23   Schematic plan views of selected Mississippian sites 36

Fig. 24   A comparison of multiple-terraced mounds and conical mounds
in the eastern U.S. 38

Fig. 25 Location of the compound and the sun circles in the Monks
         Mound area 44
Fig. 26 Plan view of circle no. 2 46
Fig. 27 Reconstructed view of a sun circle in use 47
Fig. 28 View of Murdock Mound (no. 55) in July 1941 50
Fig. 29 Relationships of early pit houses to each other 54
Fig. 30 Village occupation levels under the mound platform 57
Fig. 31 Upper village occupation levels in northeast excavation 59
Fig. 32 Circular ceremonial structure 60
Fig. 33 Ground plan and profiles of the northeast excavation 63
Fig. 34 Ground plan and profiles of the southeast excavation 64
Fig. 35 Enclosed area on mound platform 65
Fig. 36 Enclosure features 67
Fig. 37 Ground plan of mound platform 69
Fig. 38 Temple Mound faces 71
Fig. 39 Isometric reconstruction of temple mound in ritual modules 72
Fig. 40 Reconstructions of the Murdock temple mound 73
Fig. 41 Survey for construction of temple mound in two stages 77
Fig. 42 Cross sections of Murdock Mound in modules 82
Fig. 43 Pre-excavation contour map superimposed on ground plan of
         Murdock Mound 83
Fig. 44 Aerial view showing palisade lines (1933) 90
Fig. 45 Map of the central sections of the Cahokia site with palisade
         locations 91
Fig. 46 Plan view of palisade excavation showing palisade trenches 93
Fig. 47 Excavation of palisade trench showing main curtain trench of
         second palisade 96
Fig. 48 Powell Mound sherds: Holly Fine Engraved, Hickory Fine
         Engraved, and Bowles Creek Plain 104
Fig. 49 Powell Mound sherds: Holly Fine Engraved, Hickory Fine
         Engraved, and Bowles Creek Plain 105
Fig. 50 Powell Mound sherds: Holly Fine Engraved, Davis Incised, Bowles
         Creek Plain 106
Fig. 51 Powell Mound sherds: Holly Fine Engraved, Davis Incised,
         Hickory Fine Engraved 107
Fig. 52 Powell Mound sherds: Holly Fine Engraved, Bowles Creek Plain,
         Larto Red Filmed 109
Fig. 53 Powell Mound sherds: Engraved French Fork design, Holly Fine
         Engraved 111
Fig. 54 Powell Mound sherds: Crockett Curvilinear Incised, Larto Red
         Filmed, Bowles Creek Plain, Dunkin Incised, Coles Creek Incised .113

Fig. 55 Powell Mound sherds: Bowles Creek Plain 115
Fig. 56 Location of sites having corn remains 122
Fig. 57 Map of the Mitchell site 138
Fig. 58 Aerial view of the Mitchell site 142
Fig. 59 Post pit in the central portion of the Mitchell site plaza 144
Fig. 60 Bald Cypress log from the Mitchell site post pit 145
Fig. 61 Beneath Mound H, feature 47 area 147
Fig. 62 Profile of Mound H excavation 148
Fig. 63 Superimposed structures beneath Mound H 149

LIST OF TABLES

Table 1   Stratigraphic Relationships Between Soil Zones and Cultural Features. 51
Table 2   Measurements in Ritual Construction: Rectangular Coordinates. 68
Table 3   Measurements in Ritual Construction: Triangular Coordinates. . 74
Table 4   Measurements in Ritual Construction: Composite Dimensions of Rectangular and Triangular Coordinates 78
Table 5   Conversion Table to Ritual Module 80
Table 6   Relationships Indicated by Foreign Sherds from the Powell Tract Section of Cahokia 112
Table 7   Period Assignments of Mound Proveniences from Cahokia . . . 117
Table 8   Corn Found Within the Cahokia Site 124
Table 9   Corn from Sites in the American Bottom 127
Table 10   Corn from Sites Outside the American Bottom and Within 400 Miles of Cahokia 128

THE CAHOKIA SITE

Melvin L. Fowler
University of Wisconsin-Milwaukee
Milwaukee, Wis.

Introduction

Across the Mississippi River east of St. Louis is a large group of mounds. These are on the banks of a now extinct channel of the Mississippi River and between the Cahokia and Silver Creeks (Fig. 1). Located between Interstate Highways 70 & 55 and old U. S. Routes 40 & 66, these mounds and the surrounding area are passed by thousands of tourists, including many archaeologists, each year. Presently many of the mounds and the related area are in the possession of the state of Illinois and the complex is known as Cahokia Mounds State Park. This name should not be confused with the Cahokia Indians who probably had nothing to do with the archaeological site or the French village of Cahokia as the French did not even know the mounds existed.

The Cahokia site is without doubt the largest prehistoric site in North America north of Central Mexico. At present estimate it is thought to encompass over 3700 square acres (5.8 sq. Miles, 15.02 sq. Kms.) and to include within this more than 100 mounds of various sizes and shapes (Fig. 2). The largest of these features, and the one which dominates the site is Monks Mound (Fig. 3). This structure covering 15 acres of ground and rising to over 100 feet above the valley floor, is second only to Cholula and the Pyramid of the Sun at Teotihuacan in size of man–made structures in North America.

The above described dimensions of the Cahokia site, however, do not give the true picture of the complexity of this cultural occupation in this area. This is but the central group, as described by Bushnell (1904), of a much more intense or widespread occupation. This covers an area extending from Granite City, Illinois on the north to the area of Columbia, Illinois on the south. The area is the broad alluvial plain of the Mississippi River Valley known locally as the American Bottom. It has carried this name since the early part of the 19th century. In terms of the physical features the area is defined by the mouth of the Illinois River on the east side and the mouth of the Missouri River on the west side to form the northern end of the American Bottom. The southern end of the area is limited by the mouth of the

1

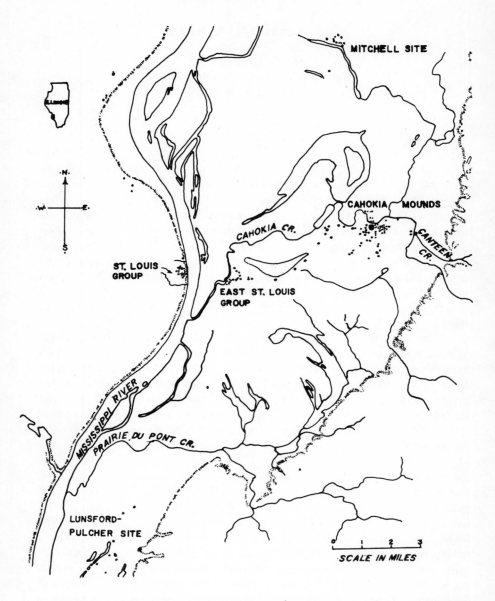

Fig. 1. A map of the American Bottom area showing the locations of sites discussed in the volume. This map is based upon Bushnell's map of 1904.

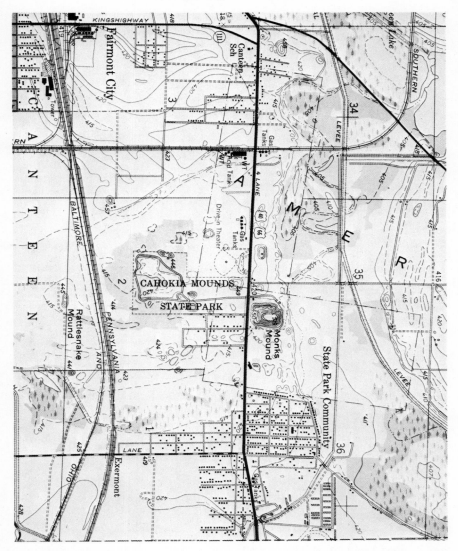

Fig. 2. The topographic map of the Cahokia Mounds archaeological site showing the extent of the site and the distribution of mounds as surveyed by the United States Geological Survey topographic mappers. This is a section of the USGS quadrangle sheet of the Monks Mound quadrangle.

Fig. 3. Two views of Monks Mound. Upper—A low oblique view of Monks Mound taken from the Southwest showing the four terraces. Lower—An oblique view from the southeast showing the first, third, and fourth terraces. Excavations on the fourth terrace are those of Washington University. Photos courtesy M. L. Fowler and Warren Wittry.

Meramac River on the west and the Kaskaskia on the east. North and south of these limits there do not appear to be any major archaeological sites for many miles. In a sense the entire American Bottom is one large Mississippian site. For example, practically every ridge of ground that extends above the flood plain contains potsherds and other indications of Mississippian occupation. These smaller sites are probably farmsteads and villages associated with the Cahokia Mounds central town.

Other than these small sites there are several large archaeological zones (see Fig. 1). Near the present town of Mitchell is a group of mounds, labeled by Bushnell the North Group, which is the basis of a paper in this volume by James Porter. At the southern end of the American Bottom area near the town of Dupo, Illinois is another group referred to as the South Group by Bushnell's map but which is now known as the Lunsford-Pulcher group. In East St. Louis, and now almost totally destroyed by urban development and highway construction, was another group of mounds probably more extensive even than the Mitchell or Lunsford-Pulcher groups. As a matter of fact it is difficult to separate this East St. Louis group from Cahokia proper as there were mounds extending along the banks of an old slough reaching from the Powell mound on the western limits of the Cahokia site into the heart of what is now East St. Louis. One of the East St. Louis mounds was described by Snyder (1919:249-250). Directly across the present channel of the Mississippi River in the heart of what is now St. Louis was another large group of mounds which also has been destroyed but was part of the overall Mississippian occupation of this area (see Williams and Goggin, 1956:7-23). However for our discussion we will limit ourselves to the Cahokia Mounds proper, or the central group in the Bushnell terminology.

I

This Cahokia archaeological zone has been well known for over 150 years having been visited by many of the early American travelers in the region. It is interesting to note, however, that the earliest detailed map we have of the area does not show the Cahokia site. This early map (Fig. 4) was made in 1796 by Gen. George Collot who undertook a journey to get information on the western portions of American territory (Tucker, 1942: Plate XXVIII). Except for the fact that the north arrow on Collot's map points northwest, it shows the features of that time in their proper relationships. For example, the mouth of the Missouri River, the locations of "St. Lewis" [sic] and the French village of Cahokia, the position of the French Fort Chartres, and the French village of Kaskaskia near to the mouth of the Kaskaskia River,

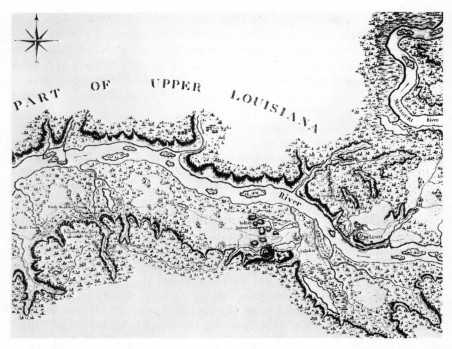

Fig. 4. A segment of the Collot map showing the location of St. Louis and the Lunsford-Pulcher site. The area of the Cahokia Mounds site is shown on the map but it does not give the location of the mounds.

are all shown in their proper relationship to each other as we know them today. In fact the area from St. Louis to Kaskaskia is shown in great detail since this is the area that the French had occupied from the early 18th century and was well traveled.

The area north of St. Louis was, in Collot's time, wilderness. The region where the Cahokia site stands is not noted except that a general prairie area is shown on Collot's map southeast of Cabaret Island, east of St. Louis, and between two creeks (probably Canteen-Cahokia and Prairie duPont Creeks). These are the proper physiographic relationships for the Cahokia site but no mounds are shown there.

This is especially interesting in view of the fact that south of St. Louis and the village of Cahokia "Indian Ancient Tombs" are shown in great detail on the map. These cannot be the Cahokia mounds as they are completely out of place. These "Tombs" probably represent the Lunsford-Pulcher site which is known today to exist in exactly that location. That it is represented on Collot's map and the much larger Cahokia site is not, is probably the result of the fact that Lunsford-Pulcher is located on the old French road leading from Cahokia to Kaskaskia.

That the French did not know about Cahokia as it was outside their path of interaction is also indicated by the fact that none of the early French explorers, LaSalle, Tonti, Marquette, who passed that way made any mention of the mounds.

George Rogers Clark who conquered the territory from the British in 1778 knew the region well but did not know of the presently named Cahokia site. Like Collot, he was well acquainted with the area south of the French village of Cahokia (Lunsford-Pulcher site) which he described as follows in his own spelling and style:

> The Indian tradition give an acct of those works they say they ware the works of their forefathers ... formerly as numerous as the Trees in the woods ... the works on the Mississippi near the Caw River is one of the largest we know of ... Kaskaskias Chief, Babtist, gave me a history of it he said that was the palace of his forefather when they covered the whole and had large towns that all those works we saw their was the Fortifications round the Town ... that the Smaller works we so (saw) far within the larger was the real palace that the little Mountain we their saw flung up with a bason on the top was a Tower that contained part of the guards ... I one day set out ... to see whether we could discover signs of such population we easily ... traced the Town for upwards of five miles in the beautifull plain below the present Town of Kokokia ... this Town appears to have occupied that part of the nearest the River but not on it as their is a strip of lower Land. Fronting nearly the sentor of this Town on the Heights in pinicle called Shugar from its figure . . . . (James, 1928: 497-498)

One of the earliest persons to give serious attention to the Cahokia mounds was Brackenridge who, in a letter to Thomas Jefferson in 1813, commented as follows:

> When I examined it in 1811, I was astonished that this stupendous monument of antiquity should have been unnoticed by any traveler: I afterwards published an account in the newspapers at St. Louis, detailing its dimensions, describing its form, position, etc. but this, which I thought might almost be considered a discovery, attracted no notice ... (Brackenridge, 1818: 154-155)

The first indication that the area of the Cahokia site was occupied by Europeans is in the report of Michael James and E. Backus, Land Commissioners and indicated that a claim for 400 acres was affirmed to Nicholas Jarrot (now locally called Jondro) on December 1st, 1809 (Hair, 1866: 37-38). In April of 1809 Jarrot donated this area to a group of Trappists monks from Kentucky who settled there and established a monastery. In 1813, due to hardship, disease, and death, they abandoned their monastery and reconveyed the land to Jarrot. The monks had built their settlements on a mound directly southwest of the main mound and gardened the first terrace of the largest mound. It was because of this brief occupation of the site by the Trappists that the largest mound is today known as Monks Mound.

In 1831, a Mr. T. Amos Hill moved onto the property and built his house on the summit of Monks Mound. He lived there for many years and reportedly was buried on the northwest corner of Monks Mound (DeHass, 1869: 297-298). A directory published in 1866 indicates that Thomas R. Ramey was the owner of the property (Hair, 1866: 190). His descendants owned the property around and including Monks Mound until it was purchased to create a state park in 1925.

Following Brackenridge's visit in 1811 there were numerous persons who, over the course of the 19th century, visited and described the site as they saw it. These records are of tremendous value to us in our studies today giving data regarding the area before it was largely destroyed by the building of highways, houses, and factories. Among these visitors were some notable persons such as Major Stephen Long and Charles Dickens.

One of the less notable, but perhaps more interesting, visitors was Micah Flint who visited the site with his father Rev. Timothy Flint in 1825. The Rev. Flint contributed descriptive details of the archaeological features while Micah was so inspired he wrote a poem, some verse of which I now quote:

> I lingered by some soft enchantment bound,
> And gazed enraptured on the lovely scene,
> From the dark summit of an Indian mound
> I saw the plain outspread of living green,
> Its fringe of cliffs was in the distance seen,
> And the dark line of Forest sweeping round.
>
> I saw the lesser mounds which round me rose;
> Each was a giant heap of mouldering clay;
> There slept the warriors, women, friends and foes,
> There side by side the rival chieftains lay;
> And mighty tribes, swept from the face of day,
> Forgot their wars and found a long repose.

(Flint, 1826: 167-168)

Some of the early visitors also appended illustrations of the area to their reports. One of the earliest of these was in 1841 (Fig. 5) and was a view looking at Monks Mound and some of the mounds south of it from the east (actually from the summit of what is now known as mound 51) (Wild, 1841: 52-53).

Featherstonhaugh (1844: 264-272) —pronounced "Fanshaw"— visited the site in 1834-1835 and made a drawing showing Monks Mound viewed

Fig. 5. A drawing of the Cahokia Mounds area published in 1841 (Wild, 1841). The artists are shown atop what is known now as Mound 51. Monks Mound is to the right of the picture. Fox Mound and Roundtop are shown to the left.

Fig. 6. A drawing of Monks Mound published in 1844 (Featherstonhaugh, 1844) viewing Monks Mound directly from the south. This drawing shows clearly the first, second, and third terraces. Of particular interest is the conical eminence on the east side of the third terrace. This has since been removed. This drawing also shows clearly that the western or left hand side of the first terrace is higher than the eastern or right hand side.

Fig. 7. A drawing of Monks Mound published by McAdams in the latter part of the 19th century. This is a view from the southwest and shows the location of Hill's home on the third terrace as well as the location of the well that Hill dug on the western slope of Monks Mound.

from the south (Fig. 6). An interesting feature of this drawing is that it shows the conical mound or eminence on the top terrace of Monks Mound which we know was graded down by Mr. Hill (See Reed, this volume, Fig. 22c). He also shows a conical mound or ridged area on the southwest corner of the first or south terrace. Evidence of this conical still exists today (see Fig. 22b). Another 19th century illustration of Monks Mound viewed from the southwest is to be found in a report made by McAdams (1882). It clearly shows the location of Hill's house and the well he had put on the western side of the mound (Fig. 7).

Whereas most of the people writing about Monks Mound and the surrounding mounds before the middle of the 19th century were writing travelogues and travel guides, those writing after that time were more interested in the archaeological features of the area. Included among these were Rau, DeHass, Putnam, and others (see Bibliography, this volume). The most detailed information we have coming from this period is from the works of

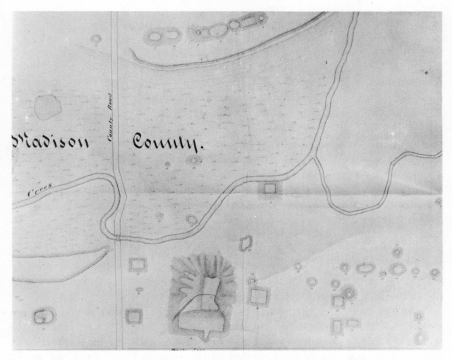

Fig. 8. The central portion of the Cahokia Mound site as mapped by A. J. R. Patrick showing the location of Monks Mound and the mounds in the immediate vicinity. Courtesy of the Missouri Historical Society.

McAdams, a local archaeologist, who had conducted excavations and reported on these in various journals. Another local amateur of this period was Dr. John Francis Snyder. For many years he was one of the leading voices promoting serious archaeological investigation of the Cahokia Site and urging its conservation as a state park (Snyder, 1913; 1914; 1917). Snyder died in 1928 just a few years before his dream became a reality.

One of the most important contributors to our knowledge of the Cahokia site in the latter half of the 19th century was Dr. A.J.R. Patrick of Belleville, Illinois. He had made, in cooperation with a local engineer, Louis Gainer Kahn, a map of the entire site area (Figs. 8 and 21). This was the first accurate map made and gave detailed locations of all the mounds and sections showing their elevations. There is no doubt but that, until the past few years, this was the best map of the Cahokia site that existed. It is now in keeping of the Missouri Historical Library in St. Louis. Several later maps were based upon the Patrick survey (e.g. Bushnell, 1904; 1922; Moorehead, 1922; 1923; 1928).

II

It was not until the 1920's that serious archaeological investigation of the Cahokia site was begun. This work was conducted by Warren King Moorehead under the auspices of the University of Illinois. Moorehead excavated into several mounds as well as other areas of the site (Moorehead, 1923, 1928). Working with Moorehead, Dr. M.M. Leighton laid to rest an earlier contention (Crook, 1915; 1916; 1918; and 1922) that the mounds were not manmade but erosional remnants (Leighton, 1928). This fanciful theory had a recent half-hearted revival (Orthwein, 1965) but has not been seriously considered since Leighton's definitive work.

During the 1920's other significant and pioneering work regarding the Cahokia site was conducted. The first aerial photographs of the Cahokia site, and probably of any archaeological site in the U.S., were taken by Army Lt. Harold Wells and Ashley McKinly. These had been requested by David I. Bushnell. A second series was taken in 1922 by Army Lts. B.W. Goddard and H.K. Ramey (Hall, 1968). These low oblique shots give excellent details of the site. Some of these were published by A.R. Crook in 1922 and prints are on file at the Illinois State Museum (see Fig. 9).

In the early part of the 1930's archaeological field work was carried out at the Cahokia site under the sponsorship of the Illinois State Museum, the Milwaukee Public Museum, the University of Chicago and the University of Illinois. This was largely concentrated at the western edge of the site in the area where a large mound, the Powell Mound, was being leveled by the landowner (Kelly, 1931; Kelly & Cole, 1933).

Another set of excellent aerial photographs of the Cahokia site were made in 1933 by Col. Dache Reeves, USAF Ret. These composed a series of three flight lines over the area and provide excellent stereo pairs and an overall mosaic of the site. These aerial photos are now preserved by the Office of Anthropology at the Smithsonian Institute (Fig. 10).

In the early 1940's, Miss Harriet Smith supervised a WPA project in the excavation of the Murdock Mound (Mound 55). This excellent work was only partially completed due to the events of Dec. 7, 1941.

Further archaeological investigations, other than the excellent records kept by devoted amateurs such as Dr. P.F. Titterington (1938) of St. Louis, were delayed by World War II. It was not until 1950 that the University of Michigan conducted work at both the Cahokia site and the Lunsford-Pulcher group (Griffin & Spaulding, 1951). In 1956 the Thomas Gilcrease Foundation sponsored excavations (Perino, 1957; 1959) in the area east of Monks Mound.

Under the direction of Preston Holder, crews from Washington University excavated in several localities in the Cahokia area. Most notably Holder and crew dug into the Kunneman mound group at the northern edge of the main Cahokia site.

Fig. 9. An aerial photograph of the Monks Mound area made by First Lieutenant Goddard in 1921 viewing the entire area from the east and looking toward the west. Monks Mound is in the central portion of the photo. Photograph courtesy of Illinois State Museum.

Fig. 10. Aerial mosaic of the Monks Mound area made by Colonel Dache Reeves (U.S. Air Force, Retired) in 1933. These are the first vertical aerial photographs we have of the Monks Mound area and show the entire site as it was before much of the modern urban expansion had destroyed the site's features. Photograph courtesy Col. Dache Reeves and the Smithsonian Institution.

The big impetus to detailed archaeological investigations at the Cahokia site came under the impact of the Federal Interstate Highway program. Interstate 70 and 55 were laid out to cut through the area just north of Monks Mound. The Illinois State Musuem, the University of Illinois, Southern Illinois University and the Illinois Archaeological Survey set up a cooperative program to salvage the data threatened with destruction by this massive construction. This program was made possible through the interest and cooperation of the United States Bureau of Public Roads and the State of Illinois Division of Highways. From 1960 to the present this cooperative salvage program has continued with the result that tremendous amounts of artifacts and other data have been accumulated. (See Fowler, 1962; 1963; 1964). In 1962, 1963 and 1964 the National Science Foundation supported research through the Illinois Archaeological Survey to analyze the data accumulated from the Interstate Highway salvage program and to conduct research on related problems. In 1964-66 Washington University sponsored research concentrating on Monks Mound.

The University of Illinois and the Illinois Archaeological Survey has continued to direct salvage archaeology in the area and also to conduct a summer field school in the Cahokia zone under the direction of Charles Bareis.

In 1966 and 1968 the National Science Foundation granted research funds to the University of Wisconsin-Milwaukee for a four year project devoted to properly mapping the Cahokia Mounds site and defining its characteristics.

III

Out of all of this investigation at the Cahokia site we are now beginning to gain some understanding of the nature of the community of people that the Cahokia site represents. First of all we now have a detailed knowledge of the extent of this community. It extends over an area, roughly diamond shaped with an east-west axis of 2.8 miles (4.6 km.) and a north-south axis of 2.1 miles (3.5 km.). The western-most mound of the Cahokia group was largely destroyed in 1933 and completely destroyed by construction activity in 1968. This was a large rectangular-based ridged-topped mound (Fig. 11) called the Powell Mound or Mound 46. A similarly shaped mound marks the southern limit of the site and is known as Rattlesnake Mound or Mound 66 (Fig. 12).

The eastern-most mound of the group is located on the edge of Canteen Creek. The northern-most group are the Kunneman mounds directly north of Monks Mound. Those were investigated by Moorehead in the 20's and by Preston Holder of Washington University in the 50's.

Basic to our understanding of the archaeological site is a good map of the area. The Patrick Map was previously our only detailed map. The map of the Cahokia area on the Monks Mound Quandrangle of the USGS series presents some adequate detail of the area. As a first step of the University of Wisconsin-Milwaukee project, a topographic map of the entire area was made through aerial photogrametric techniques (Fig. 13). This map, to scale of 1:2000 and with a one meter contour interval, will serve as a basis for re-locating mounds long since destroyed and studies of the relationships of physical features to each other. In conjunction with this we are making

Fig. 11. Upper—A 1922 oblique aerial photo of the Powell Mound at the western edge of the Cahokia site. Notice the ridge-top effect, which is oriented east-west. Photograph courtesy Illinois State Museum. Lower—An oblique photograph of the Rattlesnake Mound at the southern limits of the Cahokia Site.

Fig. 12. A ground level photograph of the Powell Mound taken from the south. Notice the depression in the left hand side which is the area of Moorehead's excavation in this mound in the 1920's.

historical and ground reconnaissance surveys to locate all of the mounds previously destroyed and other features earlier reported. Surveys indicate that, for example, the site contained within its confines over 100 mounds rather than the 85 recorded by Moorehead.

Of course, we do not know as yet how much of this area was occupied at any one time or how many of the mounds were contemporary. One of our basic concerns at the Cahokia site is the development of a chronological framework which will allow us to grapple with such problems. One thing is certain as a result of recent work and that is that the Trappist-Old Village dichotomy is much too gross and oversimplified for dealing with such problems of settlement size, pattern and history.

Several types of data have been forthcoming in the past few years that have caused a revision of previous understanding of Cahokia. In sum, these data indicate that the site was much more complex and extensive than earlier studies proposed. Wittry's excavation, under salvage conditions in areas just west of the Monks Mound area yielded some several hundred features, for example, within an area of 15 acres. Not only were there many features but there were indications that areas had been used for different functions through time.

One of the more intriguing results of Wittry's work was his discovery of features known as post pits in circular patterns. His analysis of these large circles, 240 to 480 feet in diameter, is that they were probably set up by the Indians as observatories for noting such phenomenon as the rising of the sun at summer solstice. He has named these structures "woodhenges" (see Wittry's

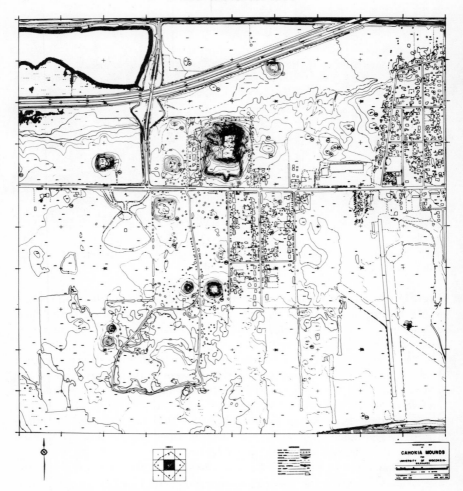

Fig. 13. The central section of the map of the Cahokia Mound site made by the University of Wisconsin-Milwaukee. The contour interval is one meter. This is the most detailed map to date of the Cahokia Mounds site.

paper in this volume). This certainly suggests that the residents of the Cahokia site were well acquainted with horizon calendars and were sophisticated enough in arithmetic and engineering to lay out such circles and make such observations.

Recently other data has come to light bearing on this same aspect of the Cahokia culture. The University of Wisconsin-Milwaukee began a project to classify the various mounds at the site in terms of their form in order to see if the distribution of the forms might suggest functional areas or differences.

One of the things we noticed was that at the western and southern limits of the site, as we understand it today, were large mounds with rectangular bases and ridged summits. These are the Powell and Rattlesnake mounds mentioned earlier. These mounds also fall on north-south and east-west axes in relationship to Monks Mound. These data suggest that the ridge top mounds were possibly a type of structure built as a monument to mark such an important point in the community as the limits or major axes. We looked for other ridge top mounds and found one south of Monks Mound and on the same north-south line as was formed by Rattlesnake and Monks Mound. This mound is known, for some mysterious reason, as Pottery Mound. On Moorehead's 1928 map of the site it is given the number 72. We follow Moorehead's numbering. Mound 72 has the ridge topped shape but instead of being oriented with the long axis east and west, as are the other ridge topped mounds in the site, it is oriented approximately 30 degrees north of west.

In studying the orientation and location of Mound 72 in relationship to other mounds and features at the Cahokia site it became obvious that it was built on a point that was not only on a major north-south axis of the site but related to other mounds to the west and east as well. Figure 14 illustrates the complex relationships that tie into Mound 72. There seemed to be one point at the southeast end of this mound that was the convergence loci of most of these relationships. It was therefore determined to excavate at that point. Upon excavation we found a large post pit that indicated the location of a large post (Fig. 15). The post had been removed but the size of the pit indicated that the post was nearly a meter in diameter and had been sunk into the ground about 2.5 meters. In preparing for the post to be put in place the Indians had positioned smaller logs in the pit to serve as cribbing (Fig. 16). Although the main log had been removed, the cribbing logs remained providing us with material for radio-carbon assays. These tests have been run by the University of Wisconsin laboratory and reported back to me as A.D. 980±50 and A.D. 930±50.

Once the post had been removed, and the reason for its removal is not known, the pit was filled in and a small domed-shaped mound built over the area (Fig. 17). Within this mound were two groups of burials. The central group was composed of several individuals ranging in age from 18 to 43. There seemed to be no doubt that the main figure of this group was the central individual who was laid out on a platform of cut shell beads (Fig. 18).

Southwest of this central group were six extended burials and three bundle burials. The six individuals, three male and three female had been buried at the same time as the central group (Fig. 19). They ranged in age from 17 to 21. Their relationship to the central figure and the restricted age range suggest to me that the six individuals were retainers sacrificed at the time of the burial of the individual on the shell platform.

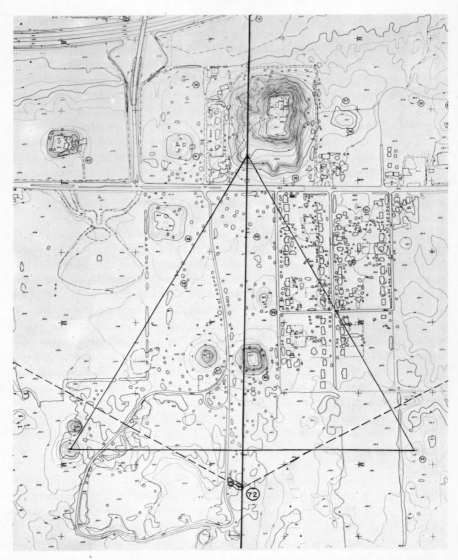

Fig. 14. The central section of the Cahokia Mounds site showing the location of Mound 72 and certain alignments of mounds relating to Mound 72 and to Monks Mound. Note particularly the point where the dashed lines intersect with the north-south line at Mound 72 and the point of the apex of the triangle on the first terrace of Monks Mound.

Fig. 15. The appearance of the post pit at the eastern end of Mound 72 is illustrated in this picture. The post pit was at exactly the location illustrated in Figure 14 of the dashed lines intersecting the major north-south line at the eastern end of Mound 72.

The grave goods accompanying these six retainers were of particular interest. These included a roll of sheet copper, 19 finely wrought chunky stones, about two bushels of uncut mica, and two caches of projectile points (Fig. 20). The projectile points are perhaps most interesting. One of the caches was placed near the head of an individual and contained over three hundred arrowheads of various forms. The other cache was across the lower legs of another individual and was made up of over 400 points.

Two very interesting factors regarding these points are to be noted. One is that they are neatly sorted into types any archaeologist would recognize both in terms of form and material. Whether the Cahokians debated about the

Fig. 16. Two views of the excavation of the post pit at the eastern end of Mound 72. Upper—shows the outlines of the pits and the marking in the bottom of the pit where the post had been standing. Lower—shows the bottom of the pit excavated and the cribbing logs that held the post in place. Photo courtesy Illinois State Museum.

Fig. 17. The primary mound surface as exposed by excavation in the eastern end of Mound 72. This primary mound was built immediately over the post pit illustrated in Figures 15 and 16.

significance of the typology, as do archaeologists, is a question that awaits further data. The other interesting factor is that some of the projectile point forms and materials from which they were made suggest relationships with the Caddo area, some with Tennessee, and some with Wisconsin. Thus, in this one burial group are stylistic suggestions of the outside ties of the Cahokia community.

These status burials suggest something about the level of social organization at the Cahokia site. What the status of the central individual of this burial group was is unknown. It certainly was sufficient to rate an attendant type burial. Due to the close juxtaposition of his burial mound over the post pit, I suspect that his status may well have been involved in factors connected with that post.

There is little doubt in my mind that the Cahokia site was carefully planned and that we are beginning to get some insights into its arrangement. Part of the significance of this arrangement had to do with horizon calendars and the major axes of the site itself.

Fig. 18. The central burial of the primary mound at the eastern end of Mound 72. This individual was an extended burial with several retainers. Some of these retainers were extended burials, some were bundle, and some were merely femurs and portions of pelves. The shell beads form a blanket or platform upon which this individual was placed. They seem to have been placed in several different groups rather than as a single unit. Underneath the shell beads is a second extended individual.

Fig. 19. A group of six burials to the southwest of the central person buried in Mound 72. These six individuals seem to have been buried as retainers to the central figure. Note the caches of projectile points, the chunky stones, the sheet copper, and the mica buried with these individuals. After these individuals were placed in the ground and the mound built over them, a pit was dug into the ground and three bundle burials (upper central portion of picture) were placed over the mica area. Photo courtesy Illinois State Museum.

Fig. 20. One of the caches of arrowheads buried with the six individuals in Mound 72. These arrowheads are neatly sorted and represent different types and materials suggesting a wide range of connections for people at the Cahokia site at this time.

IV

There are many problems of research yet to be done. Among these are efforts directed toward solving the problem of the population size of the community at any one time, the nature of the community in terms of how space was utilized and organized, and the type of economic base which supported it. We can also say something in the future about the levels of engineering and political skills of the Cahokians as a result of these studies. Then it will be possible to say more about the hinterland immediately dominated by such a community and perhaps something of the nature of the relationship of Cahokia to other similar communities in North America. The following papers will report about some of the research leading toward these goals.

At the present time we find ourselves awed by the complexity of the archaeological site of Cahokia and the communities it represents. Our feeling is akin to that of Brackenridge when he walked across the American Bottoms from St. Louis and saw the Cahokia site and Monks Mound for the first time in 1811. He said, "What a stupendous pile of earth."

References Cited

Brackenridge, Henry Marie
   1814 *Views of Louisiana together with a Journal of a Voyage up the Missouri River, in 1811.* Pittsburgh. (Modern edition published 1962 by Quandrangle Books, Inc., Chicago).
   1818 On the Population and Tumuli of the Aborigines of North America. In a Letter from H. M. Brackenridge, Esq. to Thomas Jefferson — Read Oct. 1, 1813. *Transactions of the American Philosophical Society,* Vol. 1 (New Series) pp. 151-159. Philadelphia.
Bushnell, David I. Jr.
   1904 The Cahokia and Surrounding Mound Groups. *Papers of the Peabody Museum of American Archaeology and Ethnology* (1904-1913), Vol. III, No. 1, pp. 3-20. Harvard University, Cambridge.
   1922 Archaeological Reconnaissance of the Cahokia and Related Mound Groups. Explorations and Field Work of the Smithsonian Institution in 1921. *Smithsonian Miscellaneous Collections,* Vol. 72, No. 15, pp. 92-105. Washington.

Crook, A.R.

    1915 Origin of Monks Mound. *Bulletin of the Geological Society of America,* Vol. 26, pp. 74-75.

    1916 The Composition and Origin of Monks Mound. *Transactions of the Illinois Academy of Science,* Vol. 9, pp. 82-84. Springfield.

    1918 Additional Note on Monks Mound. *Bulletin of the Geological Society of America.* Vol. 29, pp. 80-81.

    1922 The Origin of the Cahokia Mounds. *Bulletin of the Illinois State Museum.* Springfield.

DeHass, W.

    1869 Archaeology of the Mississippi Valley. *Proceedings of the American Association for the Advancement of Science. 17th Meeting held at Chicago, Illinois, Aug., 1868.* pp. 288-302. Joseph Lovering, Cambridge.

Featherstonhaugh, G.W.

    1844 *Excursion through the Slave States.* Vol. 1. London and New York.

Flint, Timothy

    1826 *Recollections of The Last Ten Years, Passed in Occasional Residences and Journeyings in the Valley of the Mississippi, from Pittsburg and the Missouri to the Gulf of Mexico, and from Florida to the Spanish Frontier; in a Series of Letters to The Rev. James Flint, of Salem, Massachusetts.* Cummings, Illiard, and Company, Boston.

Fowler, Melvin L. (Editor)

    1962 First Annual Report: American Bottoms Archaeology, July 1, 1961-June 30, 1962. *Illinois Archaeological Survey.* Urbana.

    1963 Second Annual Report: American Bottoms Archaeology, July 1, 1962-June 30, 1963. *Illinois Archaeological Survey.* Urbana.

    1964 Third Annual Report: American Bottoms Archaeology, July 1, 1963-June 30, 1964. *Illinois Archaeological Survey.* Urbana.

Griffin, James B., and Albert C. Spaulding

    1951 The Central Mississippi Valley Archaeological Survey, Season 1950 — A Preliminary Report. *Journal of the Illinois State Archaeological Society,* Vol. 1, No. 3 (new series), pp. 74-81. Fairbury, Illinois.

Hair, James T. (compiled and published by)

    1866 *Gazetteer of Madison County.* S.V. Crossman and Company, Printers. Alton, Illinois.

Hall, Robert L.

    1968 The Goddard-Ramey Cahokia Flight: A Pioneering Aerial Photographic Survey. *The Wisconsin Archeologist,* Vol. 49, No. 2 (new series), pp. 75-79. Milwaukee.

James, James Alton
    1928 *The Life of George Rogers Clark.* University of Chicago Press, Chicago.

Kelly, A.R.
    1933 Some Problems of Recent Cahokia Archaeology. *Transactions of the Illinois State Academy of Science.* Vol. 25, No. 4, pp. 101-103. Springfield.

Kelly, A.R., and Fay-Cooper Cole
    1931 Rediscovering Illinois. *Blue Book of the State of Illinois 1931-1932.* pp. 328-334. Springfield.

Leighton, M.N.
    1928 The Geological Aspects of Some of the Cahokia (Illinois) Mounds. *University of Illinois Bulletin 26,* No. 4, part 2, pp. 109-143. Urbana.

McAdams, William
    1882 Antiquities. *In History of Madison County, Illinois,* pp. 58-64. W.R. Brink & Co., Edwardsville, Illinois.

Moorehead, Warren K.
    1923 The Cahokia Mounds: Part I A Report of Progress by Warren K. Moorehead and Part II Some Geological Aspects by Morris Leighton. *University of Illinois Bulletin,* Vol. 21, No. 6. University of Illinois, Urbana.
    1928 The Cahokia Mounds. *University of Illinois Bulletin 26,* No. 4. University Illinois, Urbana.

Orthwein, Walter E.
    1965 Tests Show Monks' Mound Not Wholly Man-Made. *St. Louis Globe-Democrat,* Sept. 28, 1965. 3A. St. Louis.

Perino, Gregory
    1957 Cahokia. *Central States Archaeological Journal,* Vol. 3, No. 3, pp. 84-88. Quincy, Illinois.
    1959 Recent Information from Cahokia and Its Satellites. *Central States Archaeological Journal.* Vol. 6, No. 4, pp. 130-138. Quincy, Illinois.

Snyder, John Francis
    1913 *The Prehistoric Mounds of Illinois.* Published by "The Monks of Cahokia." 1913.
    1914 Prehistoric Illinois – The Great Cahokia Mound. *Illinois State Historical Society Journal,* Vol. 6, pp. 506-508. Springfield.
    1917 The Great Cahokia Mound. *Illinois State Historical Society Journal.* 1917-1918, Vol. 10, pp. 256-259. Springfield.
    1919 "Certain Indian Mounds Technically Considered" in *John Francis Snyder: Selected Writings,* edited by Clyde C. Walton, pp. 249-250. The Illinois State Historical Society, Springfield.

Tucker, Sara Jones (compiled by)
   1942 *Indian Villages of the Illinois County, Vol. II, Scientific Paper, Illinois State Museum. Part I, Atlas.* State of Illinois, Springfield.
Wild, J.C.
   1841 *The Valley of the Mississippi; Illustrated in a Series of Views.* Chambers and Knapp, St. Louis.
Williams, Stephen and John M. Goggin
   1956 The Long-nosed God Mask in Eastern United States. *The Missouri Archaeologist,* Vol. 18, No. 3, pp. 1-72. Columbia, Missouri.

MONKS AND OTHER MISSISSIPPIAN MOUNDS

Nelson A. Reed
Washington University
St. Louis, Mo.

Monks Mound

Monks Mound (see Figs. 3, 21, and 22) is the principal mound of the Cahokia group and the largest earthen mound in the United States, measuring approximately 1037 feet north-south, 790 feet east-west, and is 100 feet high. It is traditionally described as being built in four terraces which are numbered from the lowest to the highest. The first terrace extends across the south face of the mound at an average height of 38.5 feet and has an access ramp facing south (Fig. 22a). This is in alignment with the north-south axis of the third and fourth terraces, and is therefore offset to the east in relationship to the length of the first terrace. On the western side of the first terrace there is a rise, first tested by James Porter and then partially excavated by the University of Wisconsin-Milwaukee, under Melvin Fowler and Elizabeth Benchley. This has proved to be a square or rectangular platform built in a number of successive stages (Fig. 22b). The so-called "second terrace," is an irregular mass on the western side of the mound made up of deep ridges and gullies and a partially level area 65.5 feet high. Presently unpublished excavations at its base suggest that it is not the product of erosion, but that it is the same as when it was left by its builders (compare, for example, Fig. 21 and 22). The third terrace, 131 by 156 feet with a height of 96 feet, occupies roughly half of the top of the mound. A conical mound (Fig. 22c) some ten feet high, once stood at its southeast corner but it was leveled in 1831 by Amos Hill, a farmer who built his house on top of the mound. The fourth terrace, 194 by 156 feet with a height of 100 feet, occupies the north half of the summit. There are two projections on the east face of the mound extending from ground level to this terrace which are probably access ramps (Fig. 22d, e).

Solid core borings which penetrated 109 feet, revealing human activity all the way down to the sterile sand beneath the mound, have demonstrated that Monks Mound is entirely man-made, a point disputed by parsons, doctors and geologists for the past century. Interpretation of these cores suggests that the mound was built in fourteen stages and Carbon 14 dates give an estimated time of construction from A.D. 900 to A.D. 1200 (Reed, Bennett, and Porter,

31

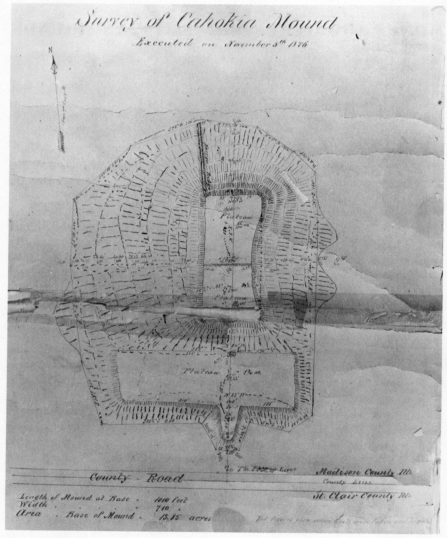

Fig. 21. The Patrick map of Monks Mound made in November of 1876. This map shows clearly the dimensions of Monks Mound as it was in Patrick's time. Patrick's estimate of the area as 13.85 acres is much less than any more recent estimate of the area covered by the mound area surface. Courtesy Missouri Historical Society.

1968). The earlier date is the beginning of the Mississippian period at the site according to contemporary thinking. Excavations of the fourth terrace by James W. Porter (Fig. 22f) found evidence of a large wall trench structure running 131 feet across the width of the terrace, its east wall running 68 feet before being interrupted by the slump of the north face. A series of not fully understood post pits were found within this structure. Wall trenches of two houses were found at the southeast corner of it, traces of stockades and post pits were found around the edge, and a major post pit, 12.5 feet below its living surface was found in the center of the terrace.

There were no structural features found in the top 70 centimeters of the extensive excavations on the fourth terrace or in the single test trench of the third terrace. Part, but not all, of the reason for this lack could be the historical activity or the destructive action of the humus. Apparently these two terraces received a final cap of earth which was not built upon. This, together with the unfinished nature of the second terrace suggests that work on the mound was interrupted in an incomplete stage, never to be completed. The terminal date of A.D. 1200 is the time period of the palisade, reported by Anderson in this volume, and military preoccupation might be one reason for the end of the great work. Nine of the ten mounds at Cahokia for which there are any data, appear to have been built after the completion of Monks Mound, or while it was in its final stage. If further work supports the idea that after two centuries of labor on a central and dominant mound, the Cahokians abandoned this mound in an incomplete state and turned to the construction of many smaller mounds, then we will have identified a major turning point in the social organization of the site.

Monks Mound is unique in size and complexity, but it is the product of a culture and the physical expression of construction principles of religious and political systems common to the Mississippian peoples. With this in mind, a review was made of 131 Mississippian sites on which data was readily available, to test theories that had developed from work on the mound.

Orientation of Principal Mounds

Monks Mound has an axis running five degrees to the east of north, an orientation repeated in a number of surrounding mounds, houses and the eastern stockade. Two "boundary" mounds, Number 1 and the Powell Mound (Number 46) are due east and west of a major post pit in the center of the fourth terrace. These facts, and the discovery of a series of large circles of post pits at Cahokia, called Woodhenges by Wittry (in this volume), suggest a Mississippian interest in celestial orientation.

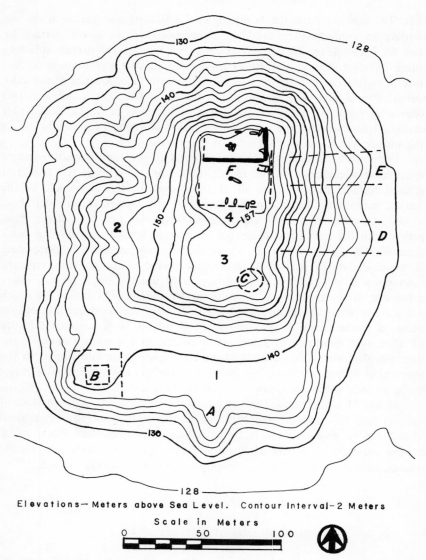

Elevations—Meters above Sea Level.   Contour Interval-2 Meters

Scale in Meters

Fig. 22. A topographic map of Monks Mound showing the location of particular features. The arabic numerals represent terraces. The letters of the
alphabet, specific features: A. The ramp of the first terrace; B. The pyramidal
mound on the southwest corner of the first terrace being excavated by the
University of Wisconsin-Milwaukee; C. The location of the conical mound that
used to be on the third terrace; D and E. Possible ramps on the eastern side
of Monks mound; F. The location of excavations by Washington University,
which revealed a structure on the fourth terrace and a large post.

One hundred and thirty-one principal mounds from a series of archaeological sites in the southeastern United States were examined for any possible pattern. The sites were drawn from the compilations of Potter (1880), Thomas (1894), and Phillips, Ford, and Griffin (1951), and individual site reports cited below. Erosian blurs the picture to a minor extent, but since most of them were rectangular, it was possible to measure their orientation within a few degrees. Of the mounds considered, there was no meaningful cluster or orientation. Upon examination, it became obvious that their layout was a result of the mound's relationship to the plaza and the surrounding environment. With respect to this point, 54 sites were relevant and available for study. Of these, 45 were laid out in conformity with the orientation of a river, slough or ridge, 7 were not affected, and two were in apparent opposition to the environmental alignment.

A basic Mississippian trait is the arrangement of mounds around a plaza which dictates that mounds will be at right angles to each other or in alignment with each other. In a number of cases, domestic structures have been found to take their orientation from the somewhat casual placement of the principal mound. Thus the east-west and five degrees to the east of north arrangement at Cahokia appears to be the product of Cahokia Creek and chance, not astronomy. Some examples (Fig. 23), of the environmentally controlled sites are Toltec (Knapp) (Thomas, 1894: Pl. x), Kincaid (Cole et al. 1952), Anna (Jennings, 1952: Fig. 142) and Saint Louis (Bushnell, 1904), while Moundville (Moore, 1905) seems unaffected by the nearby river, and Angel (Black, 1967) is in opposition to its environment. In Figure 23 one cross gives the natural alignment, while the second gives the site alignment of the principal mound of the site.

Principal Mound-Plaza Arrangement

Plazas are located to the east and south of Monks Mound. Is there a normal pattern for principal mound-plaza relationship, and can Cahokia's original or main plaza be inferred from this pattern? Of the 131 sites surveyed on this point, 102 lay in an arc SW-W-NW of their plazas, 16 were to the north, three to the south, ten on an arc NE-E-SE, and five were uncertain. The largest number, 37, were due west, the smallest number 2, were due east. Of the 16 sites with mounds to the north, 13 were near the confluence of the Ohio and Mississippi Rivers. This might be a regional or temporal variation. In general then, the trend was to place principal mounds to the west of the plaza with no effort at cardinal precision and other locations being acceptable.

No firm statement can be based on these data for Cahokia except to mention the possibility that the first plaza might have been to the east of Monks Mound. This theory gains support from the two apparent ramps on the

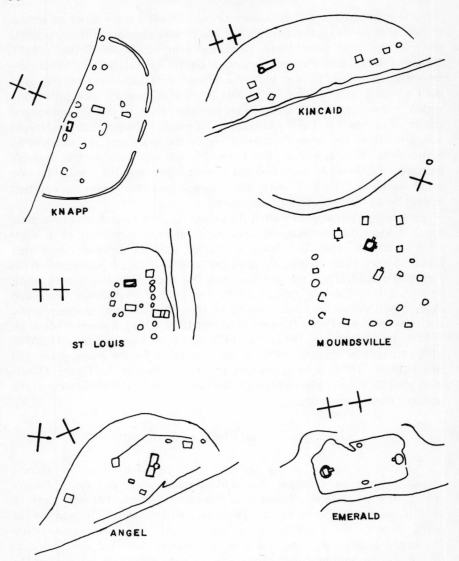

Fig. 23. Schematic plan views of various Mississippian sites in the eastern U.S. One x indicates the orientation of the principal mound of the site; the other one, the orientation of the natural surroundings of that locality.

east face (Figs. 22d and e) as all principal mounds with ramps have their ramps on the plaza side. If this was in fact the case, the orientation of Monks Mound was later changed to the south, as shown by the main south ramp and the long axis orientation of the main structure on the fourth terrace. Few large Mississippian mounds have been excavated, but such mounds as Mound F at Angel (Black, 1967), Mound C at Natchez (Neitzel, 1965), the Domiciliary Mound at Bessemer (DeJarnette and Wimberly, 1941), Mound 37 at Hiwassee (Lewis and Kneberg, 1946: Pl. 7), and Mound 6 at Obion (Kneberg, 1952: Fig. 106), have the long axis of their structures parallel to their presumed plaza.

Multi-Terraced Mounds

Monks Mound has at least three terraces, therefore the role of multi-terraced mounds was examined. Multi-terraced mounds are not particularly common, only 28 appearing in the survey (see Fig. 24). All but two of these, Richwoods (Thomas, 1894: 223) and Saint Louis, were the principal mounds at their site, and no site had more than one terraced mound. The basic form is rectangular in plan with a lower and upper stage, Cahokia and Saint Louis being the only examples of three stage mounds. A variation is with the upper stage being not as wide as the lower stage as at Old Town (Thomas, 1894: Fig. 142), where it is placed in a corner; or Clarksdale (Thomas, 1894: Fig. 158), where it is surrounded by the lower stage on three sides. The multi-terraced mounds are normally placed with the long axis parallel to the plaza. Of the non-terraced rectangular mounds on which sufficient information was available, eight were placed with long axes parallel to the plaza, while the ninth, Saint Louis's Falling Garden, isn't on the plaza. This agrees with Ford's statement about small ceremonial centers in his survey, that is, that rectangular mounds are so arranged.   This placement reinforces the earlier suggestion that Monks Mound originally faced towards a plaza on its east.

Charnel Temples, Chiefs and Burial Mounds

Truncated pyramidal mounds are often referred to as temple mounds without any evidence as to their actual function. The term "temple" by itself is unfortunate, giving false associations of a Mesoamerican flavor. Flat top mounds arranged around a plaza are both the hallmark of the Mississippian period and the principal argument for Mexican influence. In fact, an excellent argument can be made for an indigenous development of these two traits together with superficial convergence. Webb and Snow (1945), Krieger (Newell

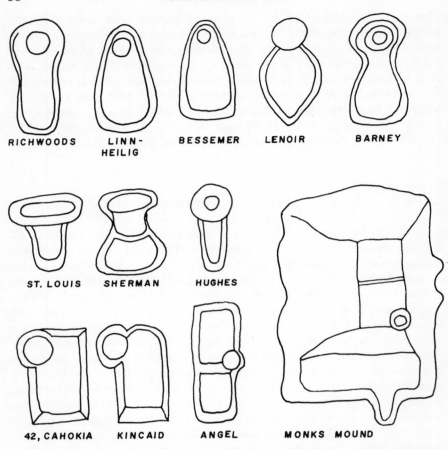

RICHWOODS   LINN-   BESSEMER   LENOIR   BARNEY
             HEILIG

ST. LOUIS   SHERMAN   HUGHES

42, CAHOKIA   KINCAID   ANGEL   MONKS MOUND

Fig. 24. A comparative representation of the multiple-terraced mounds and conical mounds in the eastern U.S.

and Krieger, 1949), and Webb and Baby (1966) have shown that the basic religious symbols of eastern ceremonialism (Southern Cult, another diffusionist gold mine) have Adena-Hopewell ancestry. The same can be said for the functional essence of the charnel-temple mound. Charnel houses were built on platforms by the Adena-Hopewell for the custom of bone picking or exposure of the dead. After the process was completed, the building was usually burned and then covered over with a mantle of earth. This would be necessary to protect the bones from animals or enemies at a seasonally occupied site. The absence of the earth covering, no longer necessary in a permanent town where a guard could be maintained year round, and a larger platform is all that is necessary to transform this type of Adena-Hopewell burial mound into a

Mississippian Charnel-temple mound. Platform mounds, as such, apparently existed among various pre-Mississippian cultures such as Hopewell, Crystal River and Weeden Island. As the dead elite were honored by a mound, it would seem an easy and natural step to so honor the living ruler, and build his house on a nearby mound. The area between these two mounds would be the obvious place for religious celebration, since it is kept free of domestic structures. It is in this way that a plaza is formed.

The focal point is the Charnel-Temple. The idols inside and the carved figures on either side of the door as reported in the ethnographic literature were not to be worshiped (see Garcilaso de la Vega, 1951). They were to commemorate and protect the bones of the communities' past rulers, their families and retainers. A victor's first act in a conquered town was to scatter and defile these bones. The sacred fire of the "temples" can be compared to the funeral fire associations of the southeast, and the riches described in these buildings can be compared with funeral offerings. All of this is quite unlike anything found in Mexico. DeSoto saw these charnel-temples from Florida to Arkansas. Such a geographic spread among tribal and language groups implies a considerable depth in time for this trait, presumably the entire Mississippian period. There is still the probability of much influence from Mesoamerica that came with the transmission of corn, but not necessarily on a late time period.

Archaeological evidence offers little to differentiate between the charnel-temple and the status residence mound. Neitzel's (1965) work at the Fatherland site, the chief town of the Natchez, reveals the difficulties at even that well-described site. In DeSoto's time at least, both types of structures existed in capital and village. The charnel-temple was sometimes, but not always, larger and construction techniques were the same. Both had ramps, hearths and beds against the wall, in the one case to hold coffins. At Fatherland, the charnel-temple was to the west of the plaza. Burial in the floor of a house is known, and the bones in baskets or chests of the classical charnel-temple would presumably be scattered and not found in the mound. A possible lead is to consider the various burial mound shapes. They were conical, hemispheric or rectangular in plan and while submounds might be flat, the final form was rounded. This is the easiest to build and the most resistant to erosion.

The pairing of truncated mounds and conicals is found at Cahokia as a pattern, Mounds 57-60 and 67-68 (see Fig. 13), and there were four such pairs on the Sikeston Ridge in Missouri (Potter, 1880). There is no regular orientation of these pairs, and they seem independent of the plaza-forming process. It has been suggested that the truncate held a charnel-temple where bodies were left for a certain period of time and were later to be buried in the conical mound which grew by accretion. This is reported by Adair (Swanton,

1931) of the Choctaw. Another possibility would be to pair the house mound of the chief or lineage leader with the burial mound for the status dead of that group.

A compound type of mound, the truncate with conical, offers suggestive possibilities. This type is the principal mound at Kincaid, Angel, Bessemer, Linn-Heilig (Lynn) (Thomas, 1894: Fig. 82), Richwoods and Lenoir (Thomas, 1894: Fig. 278), with other examples at Sherman, Barney, Hughes (Thomas, 1894: Figs. 132, 145, 151), Saint Louis, Mound 42 at Cahokia, and a mound on the bluffs of Madison County, Illinois. In some cases, such as Linn-Heilig, Lenoir, and Bessemer, burials have been found in the conical. In three cases tested, Kincaid, Bessemer and Angel, the conical is a later addition to the truncate. This class appears to bridge the gap between the burial and the charnel-temple mound, and as such, suggests the associations of its class. As mentioned, Monks Mound originally had a conical with burials in it, and by this reasoning could be a variant of the charnel-temple type.

Summary

1. There is no regular pattern of celestial orientation of principal mounds. Mississippian sites are laid out in relationship to their environment, usually a river or slough. Because of the plaza forming process, mounds have an intra-site orientation, parallel or at right angles, based on the random orientation of the principal mound.

2. Principal mounds are usually to the west of their plaza with no cardinal precision, although other locations are acceptable, with a cluster of sites having a northern placement near the Mississippi-Ohio confluence.

3. Multi-terraced mounds are relatively rare, only one per site. Normally they are the principal mound and are placed with their long axis parallel to the plaza. This last point is also true of one-stage rectangular mounds.

4. The indigenous nature of the charnel-temple mound is emphasized as opposed to the diffusionist approach, with Mesoamerican connections on the Mississippian time period. Ethnography reports this and status residence as functions for truncate mounds but offers little in structural detail with which to differentiate between them in excavation.

5. Truncates with conical mounds appear to be a combination of structure platform and burial mound. They are often the principal mound at their site.

6. Because of the western location, the long axis parallel, and the two probable eastern ramps, it is suggested that Monks Mound originally faced a plaza to its east, an orientation which was later changed to the south. If true, it would be interesting to know the significance in such a change. It is also

suggested that because of the conical (Fig. 22c), Monks Mound served as a charnel-temple during at least one period of its complex history. It will take deep and massive excavations to test these theories.

References Cited

Black, Glenn A.
    1967 *Angel Site, An Archaeological, Historical, and Ethnological Study.* Indiana Historical Society, Indianapolis.
Bushnell, David I., Jr.
    1904 The Cahokia and Surrounding Mound Groups. *Papers of the Peabody Museum of American Archaeology and Ethnology,* Vol. 3 (No. 1), pp. 3-20.
Cole, Fay-Cooper and others
    1951 *Kincaid, A Prehistoric Illinois Metropolis.* University of Chicago Press, Chicago.
DeJarnette, David L. and Steve B. Wimberly
    1941 The Bessemer Site. *Geological Survey of Alabama, Museum Paper* 17.
Garcilaso de la Vega, G.S.
    1951 *The Florida of the Inca.* Translated and edited by J.C. Varner and J.J. Varner. University of Texas Press, Austin.
Jennings, Jesse D.
    1952 Prehistory of the Lower Mississippi Valley. In: *Archeology of Eastern United States,* edited by J.B. Griffin, pp. 256-271. University of Chicago Press, Chicago.
Kneberg, Madeline
    1952 The Tennessee Area. In: *Archeology of Eastern United States,* Edited by J.B. Griffin, pp. 190-198. University of Chicago Press, Chicago.
Lewis, T.M.N. and M. Kneberg
    1946 *Hiawassee Island.* University of Tennessee Press, Knoxville.
Moore, Clarence B.
    1905 Certain Aborignal Remains Along the Black Warrior River. *Journal of the Academy of Natural Sciences of Philadelphia,* Vol. 13 (pt. 2), pp. 125-244.
Neitzel, Robert S.
    1965 Archaeology of the Fatherland Site: The Grand Village of the Natchez. *Anthropological Papers of the American Museum of Natural History,* Vol. 51 (No. 1), pp. 1-108.

Newell, H.P. and Alex D. Krieger
 1949 The George C. Davis Site, Cherokee County, Texas. *Memoirs, Society for American Archaeology*, No. 5.
Phillips, Philip, James A. Ford, and James B. Griffin
 1951 Archaeological Survey in the Lower Mississippi Alluvial Valley, 1940-1947. *Papers of the Peabody Museum of Archaeology and Ethnology*, Vol. 25.
Potter, W.B.
 1880 Archaeological Remains in Southeastern Missouri. *Contributions to the Archaeology of Missouri, Archaeological Section of the Saint Louis Academy of Science.*
Reed, Nelson A., John W. Bennett and James Warren Porter
 1968 Solid Core Drilling of Monks Mound: Technique and Findings. *American Antiquity*, Vol. 33 (No. 2), pp. 137-148.
Swanton, John R.
 1931 Source Material for the Social and Ceremonial Life of the Choctaw Indians. *Bureau of American Ethnology, Bulletin 103.*
Thomas, Cyrus
 1894 Report on the Mound Explorations of the Bureau of American Ethnology. *Twelfth Annual Report, Bureau of American Ethnology, 1890-1891.*
Webb, William S. and Raymond S. Baby
 1966 *The Adena People No. 2.* Ohio Historical Society, Columbus, Ohio.
Webb, William S. and Charles S. Snow
 1945 The Adena People. *University of Kentucky Reports in Anthropology and Archaeology*, No. 6.

THE AMERICAN WOODHENGE*

Warren L. Wittry
Cranbrook Institute of Science
Bloomfield Hills, Mich.

Several centuries ago, the largest Indian town in North America flourished on the broad fertile terrace of the Mississippi River opposite the present city of St. Louis. It was a dispersed town with hamlets, house clusters and individual houses spaced by cornfields, lakes and creeks. In five locations within the town there were large ceremonial centers with plazas and temples elevated on high earthen pyramidal mounds. This great town was no longer occupied in 1673 when Jolliet and Fr. Marquette canoed down the Mississippi. About 1698 a settlement of the Cahokia tribe was established at the mouth of a creek now called Cahokia Creek. It is from the name of this creek, which flows through the central part of the site, that the prehistoric town derives its modern name.

In its heyday, the Cahokia site represented a relatively high state of culture compared to that possessed by the Midwestern Indians at the time of the coming of the Frenchmen. Why this great town with thousands of inhabitants was abandoned shortly before the Historic Period is not known. But archaeologists are working on the solution to this problem, as well as many other problems connected with reconstructing the story of Cahokia.

A visitor to the site today cannot possibly imagine the town in its original state. If he were to climb to the top of Monks Mound in the central ceremonial group, he would see dense clouds of smoke from modern factories, acres and acres of housing development, and broad belts of concrete highways. If he were looking for them, he might discern a few high places which in former times supported the temples and chiefs' houses. Nothing else is there to remind the eye of thousands of thatched houses and peaceful cooking fires or the periodic awe-inspiring ceremonies in which, we can postulate, the entire populace participated as performer or spectator. Even the mounds have suffered the ravages of time and the forces of nature. Some have been removed by the power shovel; most of the others have been rounded by the plow; only a few retain approximately their original truncated pyramidal form (see Fig. 25).

---

*Reprinted, with minor revision from the *News Letter,* Cranbrook Institute of Science, Vol. 33, No. 9; 102-107. Bloomfield Hills, Mich.

Fig. 25. A drawing of Monks Mound area as viewed from the southwest showing the location of the specific features such as the compound and the sun circles excavated by the Illinois State Museum.

Though long a mecca for Indian relic collectors, there had been little work by professional archaeologists at Cahokia. In the 1920's Warren K. Moorehead conducted excavations during four seasons. His workmen dug mainly in mounds, but a few village and burial areas were also sampled. Fieldwork in the 1960's has been intensive because the Federal-Aid Highway Act of 1956 contained a provision for the salvaging of archaeological remains which would be destroyed by construction of certain highways. This work has been done for the most part under the auspices of the Illinois Archaeological Survey in cooperation with the Illinois Division of Highways and the U.S. Bureau of Public Roads. Subsequent analyses of the data have been partially supported by Illinois State Museum, National Science Foundation, and Cranbrook Institute of Science.

The central ceremonial group originally contained over 80 mounds. According to several radiocarbon age determinations it was occupied for at least 750 years, from about A.D. 800 until about A.D. 1550. The group was, and is, dominated by Monks Mound, the largest prehistoric earthwork in North America (see Reed, this volume). To the east, south, and west of Monks Mound there were plazas surrounded by lesser mounds. In the plaza to the west, recent excavations uncovered six successive ceremonial structures ranging from 50 to over 200 feet in diameter. That these were public, rather than private, structures is unquestioned, though their exact functions may never be known. Also within the central group, 3,000 feet west of Monks Mound, was another area which for a time was devoted to public structures (Fig. 25). Here were located, in succession, four huge circles of spaced wooden posts called "henge monuments" built during the late Neolithic Period in western Europe and England. The term "henge," apparently originally applied to the lintel or "hanging" stones at Stonehenge in England, has been extended to include other circular structures of stone or wood posts. The method of erecting the huge posts at Cahokia was exactly parallel to that used in erecting the posts and stones in Europe. I do not propose any historical connection between the European henges of the second millennium B.C. and the Cahokia henges of A.D.1000. Rather, the structures of these two areas, widely separated in space and time, do show similarities in form, method of construction and, possibly, in function. In this brief article I shall describe one of the four henge structures so far discovered at the Cahokia site.

To make a long story short, during the seasons of 1960 and 1961 we discovered a number of long oval-shaped pits which slanted downward from one end to the other. We called these pits "bathtubs" because of their general shape, and initially we were perplexed as to their function. A number of theories were proposed, but the one which we eventually adopted was that they were *post pits,* that is, pits which were dug in order to erect rather large wooden posts. The evidence for this came from the north ceremonial center near Mitchell, Illinois, where my colleague, James W. Porter, found the base of a cypress log still remaining in one of these peculiarly shaped pits (see Porter, this volume).

Some months after my 1961 fieldwork was completed, I detected that some of the scattered post pits in the area 3,000 feet west of Monks Mound could be separated into segments of perfect circles. Four such circles ranging from 240 to about 480 feet in diameter have so far been discovered. There yet remain some post pits which obviously are not parts of circles and which had some other functions, either as single posts or in combinations as yet undetermined. Post pits occur also in the larger houses and these undoubtedly contained roof supports. That the circles, however, are not a matter of my imagination is attested by the discovery of additional parts of Circle No. 2 by Dr. Robert L. Hall during the 1963 field season. The circle is believed to be the second in the sequence of four which have come to light so far. It must be pointed out that only a few acres of this vast site have been excavated, so our sample is a very small one.

Circle No. 2 can be approximately dated because one of the post pits of Circle No. 3 was superimposed on one of its post pits. A radiocarbon date on Circle No. 3 indicates that it dates to about A.D.1045 (M-1341). Thus, Circle No. 2 was built prior to that year, but probably not long before, and I have arbitrarily selected A.D.1000 as the date of Circle No. 2.

This American Woodhenge was 410 feet in diameter (Figs. 26 and 27). It was a very precise circle and most certainly was laid out with the use of a peg and rope compass. Though we uncovered only slightly less than one-half of the original circle, we can reconstruct it to have had four of its posts at the cardinal points and a total of 48 posts evenly spaced about its

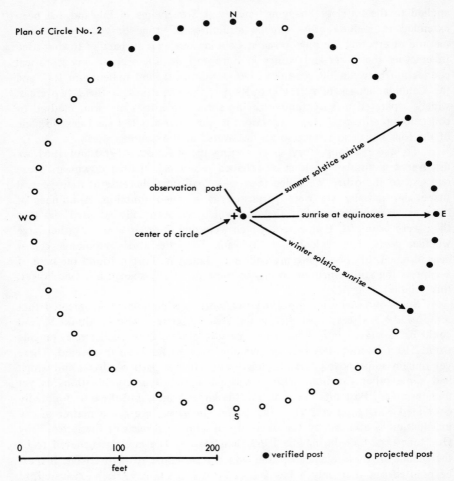

Fig. 26. A plan view of circle no. 2 excavated by the Illinois State Museum showing the alignments of some of the posts in a circle as they relate to solar calendrical observation.

circumference. The posts' pits averaged 7 feet long, 2.2 feet wide, and a little over 4 feet deep. Impressions at the deep ends, where the weight of the posts pressed the ends into the soil, showed that the posts averaged 2 feet in diameter. Posts of this size could have been relatively high, but their actual heights can only be conjectured. In the illustrations they are represented as extending about 30 feet above the surface. It is possible that earth was heaped up around their bases to give additional support.

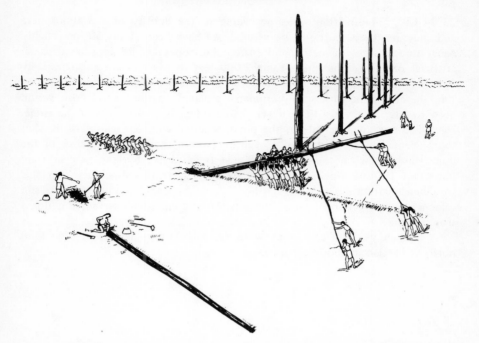

Fig. 27. This drawing illustrates the way in which a sun circle might have been constructed by the Indians. The figures at the left hand are shown excavating a post pit with a sloping ramp. The next group is inserting a post into the hole.

From the center of the circle there was an angular distance of 7°30' between adjacent posts. Dr. Hall's further exploration of the circle in 1963 also covered the area of the center, and there a post was located five feet to the east of the true center. Now this is most interesting, for an observer on this post would see slightly different angles toward the eastern side of the circle. Looking east, he would see a post in that direction, but looking at the fourth post to his left he would be looking, not 30° north of east (as he would if he were at the true center) but at an angle slightly greater than 30°.

If my calculations are correct, the angle represented from the post near the center of the circle to the second post would be the angle upon which the observer, at approximately A.D. 1000, would see the sunrise on midsummer day, the summer solstice. The variables which must be taken into account are: (1) the latitude of the observer, (2) the inclination of the ecliptic, (3) refraction, and (4) the relationship of the point of observation to the horizon.

Taking these factors into account we have (1) the latitude of the observer as North 38°39'5", (2) the inclination of the ecliptic at A.D. 1000 was

23°34'12", (3) refraction varies according to the density of the atmosphere and may for these purposes be assumed to have been about 30' or roughly equal to the sun's diameter, and (4) the horizon must be considered as an artificial one since the bluffs some 2,000 feet to the east are approximately 125 feet higher than the river bottom. To obtain a clear view of the rising sun, therefore, the observer, presumably situated on the central post, would need to have his eyes a little lower than the height of the posts of the circle.

The unknown heights of the posts, together with our ignorance of what the ancient Cahokians defined as sunrise (was it the first appearance of the upper limb or when the lower limb just touched the horizon or post?) are important factors which only allow us to suggest the possibility that this woodhenge structure and three others like it at Cahokia were used as sun calendars where observations of the solstices and equinoxes served to define a tropical year.

If such was the case, they were the only known devices of their kind north of Mexico in aboriginal America.

THE MURDOCK MOUND, CAHOKIA SITE

Harriet M. Smith
Field Museum of Natural History
Chicago

A preliminary report on Murdock Mound, Number 55 on Moorehead's map (Moorehead, 1928:9) was published in the *Journal of the Illinois State Archaeological Society* in March, 1942 (see Smith, 1942). Because of wartime restrictions it appeared in mimeographed form without any illustrations, and was not widely circulated. The editor of this volume felt that the information in the preliminary report should again be made available, along with an expanded interpretation of the data presented at the Central States Anthropological Society meetings in May of 1966. It is hoped this material will be useful in current archaeological investigations.

The excavation of the Murdock Mound was undertaken under the joint sponsorship of the Illinois State Museum, the Illinois State Division of Parks, and the Museum Extension Project, one of the professional programs of the Public Activities Division of the Works Projects Administration in Illinois. The writer directed the excavation, reporting to Dr. Thorne Deuel, Chief of the Illinois State Museum. Miss Trava Wilson, a graduate student in archaeology from the Department of Anthropology of the University of Chicago, assisted in the technical supervision for the last four months of the excavation period, which started June 11th and ended December 15, 1941.

This investigation was undertaken as a salvage job when it was learned that one of the mounds of the Cahokia group, just outside the east boundary of Cahokia Mounds State Park, was being leveled by the building of the Mounds Acreage subdivision. Mr. Murdock, owner and contractor, kindly agreed to permit excavation before the mound's destruction. Unfortunately we did not have enough time to completely investigate the mound.

Evidence will be presented on stratigraphy, structures and features, chronological relationships, and reconstruction of the mound (see Figs. 28 and 29). Little data is available on artifactual materials due to their paucity at Murdock Mound, and the lack of a pottery analysis because of a laboratory mixup.

Fig. 28. Murdock Mound, Cahokia No. 55, in July 1941. After long cultivation it stood only 9-1/2 feet above the surrounding ground surface and was
being leveled for a house site, Lot 22, of the new Murdock Subdivision.
Stripping of human bones from the light area in the foreground was reported
to the Illinois State Museum.

Stratigraphy

There were 6 major soil zones or layers comprising 16 successive ground
surfaces, 13 of which had structures on them (see Table 1).

Layer I—*Basal Clay*

At the base of the stratigraphic column to an unknown depth lies a
water-deposited clay zone that is bluish-yellow in color and putty-like in consistency. It is found over the entire subdivision 2 to 6 feet below the present
surface.

Layers II & III   weathered loess — *Village* and *Platform*

Over the base clay is a layer of weathered loess (Village zone) averaging
2 feet in thickness which was built up by a combination of village debris and
flood deposits. Within the surrounding 50 feet or so around Murdock Mound,
this weathered loess does not show up in test pits. It had been stripped off to
build, in stages, a low platform which thus consisted of the same debris as the
underlying Village layer. Therefore, scattered sherds, etc., must be assigned a
Village age. Few cultural materials were found in direct association with the
structures built on the low superimposed platforms. Eventually these house
platforms were consolidated into a 3 foot high ceremonial platform (P-8).

The village ground surface on which the platform was built could be
detected in most profiles as a structural separation which was originally

TABLE 1

STRATIGRAPHIC RELATIONSHIPS BETWEEN SOIL ZONES AND CULTURAL FEATURES

Layer	Soil Zone	Depth From Datum Plane	Formation	Form and Function	Cultural Content
I	Basal Clay	post hole base -15.2' Natural top -12.25'	water deposited	Village	V-1 double pit house, Woodland Culture.
II	Weathered Loess	top -10.7' (V-6) (1-1/2 ft. deep)	mainly cultural accretion	Village	V-2 through V-5 occupation levels. Developmental to Full Mississippi Culture.
III	Redeposited Village Loess	top -8.0' (2.7 ft. high)	consolidated house platforms (human agency)	Platform	P-3 through P-8. Status neighborhood to Civic Center, Cornerstone Pit for Temple Mound.
IV	Redeposited Gumbo	base -10.7', top +22.3' (orig. height 33 ft.)	loading by labor gangs	Temple Mound (truncated pyramid with faceted corners)	Temple debris from 13th occ. level, 8 fragmentary burials.
V	Unweathered Loess	tapering base -10.7' top ca. -8.5'	human agency	Burial Aprons	4 burial heaps at N, stripped at S, devoid of cultural material.
VI	Mixed Wash	base ca. -8.5' up to present ground surface	Deposited by erosion of Temple Mound	—	practically sterile.

designated platform level 2. Recognition of the common village base in both NE and SE excavation, placed P-3 as the earliest platform house, raised 8 inches above the surrounding V-6 surface (the finest house (P-4) used the same platform, raised another 4 inches).

Layer IV   redeposited gumbo — *Temple Mound*

A relatively sterile gumbo had been brought in to compose the temple mound (Figs. 34, 36a, and 37) which overlay the loess platform surface (Figs. 31, 37) and overlapped the town surface (Fig. 39). There were no grave goods with the 8 fragmentary "burials"; chance cultural inclusions must be regarded as coming from the source area of the gumbo.

Not dealt with in the preliminary report were the final two layers:

Layer V   unweathered loess from the Collinsville Bluffs — *Burial Aprons*

Bright loess was piled to make level, foot-high burial floors (Fig. 33, vertical section) over the tapering margin of mud wash (Fig. 30a, pedestal), and against the sharp dark mound faces at the northeast (Figs. 38a, b) and southeast (Fig. 28, foreground). More loess covered the bones and tapered off in an apron shape extending beyond the temple mound from 5 to almost 25 feet at the "corners." This loess apron sealed off the stump of the temple mound to about a 4-foot height, preserving measurable dips of slope.

The loess apron also had sealed over chunks of the wattle-and-daub wall of the Temple. These chunks had tumbled off the temple platform and come to rest on the mud wash at the base of the mound only a short time before construction of the burial apron on top of them.

Layer VI   from erosion of the Temple Mound—from above Burial Aprons up to present surface — *Mixed Wash*

Blurring the top of the Burial Apron in places, the upper two-thirds of the gumbo mound has spread over the surrounding area (Figs. 30a, 38) progressively raising it to the present ground level.

Structures and Features

Thirteen of the ground surfaces excavated in the Murdock Mound—all except the Village surface (V-6) and the burial floor in the post-mound aprons—had structures built on them.

There were six different types of structures found at various levels in the loess Village and Platform sequences. Sixteen superimposed levels (including the present ground surface) were distinguished. Of these, the earliest and next to the uppermost of the six village layers (II) and the fourth and eighth composing the loess Platform (Layer III) have been worked out completely enough to describe some architectural details of the individual structures.

Village Features
Layers I and II

Double Pit House, Woodland Culture, V-1
(Figs. 29a, b)

The close of the field season (with Pearl Harbor) did not permit complete excavation of the earliest house found. The ten feet excavated in from its north wall show this structure to have had a sub-surface floor dug 9 inches further down into the basal, putty clay zone from a clay wall bench. This bench was flat-cut inside the wall posts and slanted to the floor at about 35° from the vertical. Its edge shows little wear before a flood forced the occupants to salvage their house posts and flee. Poles 2-1/2 inches in diameter were set into this bench about a foot apart at a distance of 2-1/2 to 3 feet from its inner edge (the bench gradually widened toward the west). A large post, 8-1/2 inches in diameter, for support of the roof beams was 5 feet inside the line of wall posts and was set 18 inches deep into the basal, putty clay sub-surface floor.

This inner or floor pit was actually dug a total of 1-1/2 feet into the base clay, for the whole V-1 house was set in a sharp-rimmed outer pit dug (Figs. 29c, 32) 8 inches from the top of the base clay and extending something under 7 inches on up to an indefinite ground surface in the weathered loess—a total pit depth of about 2 feet for V-1. Just outside the line of wall posts, the wall bench surface was unsmoothed as it started sloping upward for two feet, then rose steeply to form the 7-inch high rim of this outer pit that had been "hacked" out of the base clay. Scalloped tool marks about 2 inches wide were readily trowled out by flicking away from the clay, the mica sand flood fill of the inner pit and post holes which had settled 1-1/2 inches deep over the top of the bench within the outer pit. All the posts were salvaged when the occupants abandoned their home before the rising flood waters.

The top of the flood fill was marked by a level, sparkling line of mica flecks which had settled as the flood waters, trapped in the double pit, dried.

This first occupation level was represented on the south side of the mound site as well, in a test pit, by post molds with the same glittery sand fill into the base clay.

If three post molds make an orientation line, this other V-1 house was also lined up due East-West. Apparently the posts had been set into a similar bench, for again a mica flood-line extended across a presumed pit and was 2 inches above a smooth-cut clay bench at this spot.

The minimum North-South dimension of the V-1 house—assuming that the next shovelful of pit fill would have disclosed a parallel inner supporting post also 5 feet from a corresponding south wall of the house—would be 19 feet from wall to wall and would have required an outer "pie-pan" pit (rather

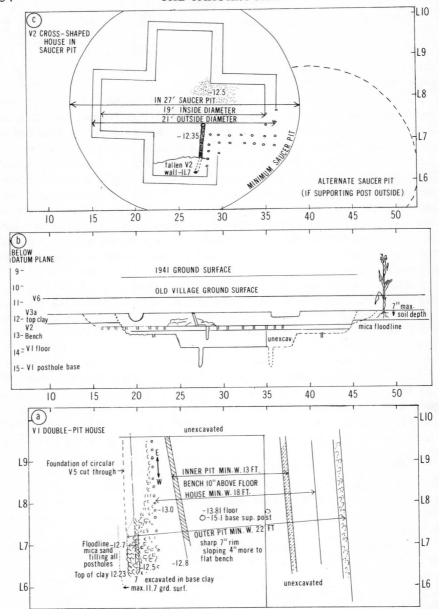

Fig. 29. Relationships of Early Pit-Houses to each Other and Ground Surfaces; (a) Bottom: ground plan of Double Pit House, V1 occupation level; (b) Middle: vertical section of village level V1 through V3a; (c) Top: ground plan of Cross-Shaped House in a saucer-pit.

than saucer) 27 feet in diameter at its intersection with the top of the base clay.

Double-Walled, Cross-Shaped Structure, V-2
(Figs. 29b, c)

The second oldest floor level under Murdock Mound is in the pit fill of V-1, 3 inches below the natural top of the surrounding base clay. Its occupants must have deliberately chosen the shallow, saucer-shaped depression some 30 feet wide that probably remained after a few spring rains washed in loess from the sharper rim of V-1's outer pit. (Fig. 29b).

This preference for depressions, along with the double walls of singly set posts, warrants a more critical comparison that I am qualified to make with the Matthews site (New Madrid focus) (Walker and Adams, 1946) in southeastern Missouri. I can point out that the rectangular Matthews houses also had double walls of singly set posts, with large inner supporting posts, and were also set in saucer-pits 30 feet wide by 2 feet deep. This is a surface site and was considered protohistoric in 1946—as, of course, was the Middle Mississippi Culture in general. If the Murdock V-2 structure was in a Matthews-type community, this area facing on Cahokia Creek to the north should have been enclosed within a ramped stockade. Such an early Cahokia community would have focused on a "Southern type" mound just about where Monks Mound stands.

I'm not sure whether this is what either of them had in mind when Wray quoted a personal communication from J.B. Griffin in his 1952 article:

"Early Mississippi, Old Village focus: Cahokia was apparently a cultural center before Old Village with a temple mound complex of southern origin which is pre-Middle Mississippian. This is combined with a utilitarian complex of Jersey Bluff type " (Wray, 1952: 159).

Establishment of a village plan from this stage on would make it no coincidence that the same building site was henceforth used for a succession of houses increasingly Mississippian in character: namely, V-3a, 3b, 4, and 5 (see Table 1).

Structures in Pits. The practice of building in pits seems a firmly established tradition as evidenced by the round ceremonial structure in the fully developed Mississippian complex of the Murdock V-5 level, a seeming retention of an ancestral local form which is represented by V-1 and V-2. The houses of the Eveland site near Dickson, Illinois, were typically set in saucer pits, both the normal rectangular residence and the unusual cross-shaped structure (Alan Harn, personal communication) which Murdock V-2 resembles in shape. Murdock V-1 may be an earlier form of the Eveland pit house, called at Dickson an earth lodge.

The northeast quadrant of the V-2 structure had been destroyed in the digging of the deep wall trench of the circular V-5 structure. The wingspread of the V-2 house, extended, should have been 23 feet on the outside, 21 inside. The double rows of wall posts were a foot apart (Fig. 29c, b). The 6 foot square alcoves in the Murdock building would be cramped for a residence, but it may have been a storehouse. Inside the west alcove there was a loess bench or a pile of stored supplies, for whatever it was, it caused the big inner supporting post to break when it fell, as charcoal, across it, and it held the broken-off part of the charred post up at an angle, as loess filled in around it up to the V-3a level.

Fire Fighting. Most of the wall posts of the cross-shaped structure did not burn (Fig. 30). It seems that in an attempt to stop the fire, the surrounding loess was thrown over the partially collapsed and still smoldering debris and that this was what kept the slanting post in place until it got sliced off horizontally 9 inches above its V-2 floor in the leveling of the floor of the V-3a house, presumably in the ground level of that time.

Most of the Murdock houses burned. The method of fire-fighting, suggested for the Kincaid site, could account for much of the accumulation not only of the 9 inches of loess between V-2 and V-3a levels, but of the next foot (three more burned house levels) to the final Village ground surface, V-6 (Smith, 1963).

Shift in Orientation. The V-1 houses were built on a true East-West line. The next structure, V-2, was lined up 10° South of East (Fig. 29), and thereafter orientation was progressively from 8° to 7-1/2° South of East for all subsequent structures on Murdock site: eight occupation levels plus both the Platform and Temple Mound. This is expressed in terms of East because I consider this shift a reflection of an intensified concern with agriculture and a more sophisticated body of astronomical knowledge related to the farmers' seasonal almanac, based on the sun.

Developmental Mississippian House Features, V-3a and V-3b
(Fig. 29b)

A small section of burned floor and a rimless fire basin, neither lined with puddled clay, scattered post molds and three shallow refuse and ash pits were found during the stepped excavation of the next 15 inches of village loess deposit (above V-2 and below V-4). These were assigned a single occupation level although they represented several stages.

Well-defined levels were V-3a at -11.7 feet and V-3b at -11.45 feet below datum. The latter is 3 inches below the V-4 house of singly set posts of the type called "Early Kincaid" at that site.

Fig. 30. Village Occupation Levels under Platform. Upper—Workman kneeling on V1 wall bench removes sample of V2 supporting post. Lower—Flood fill of mica sand in V1's floor pit; Double walls of V2 with wall trench of V5 residence cutting through step above it; Platform facet.

Vestibule House with Singly-Set Wall Posts, V-4
(Fig. 31a, inner wall lines)

The next definitive alignment of post molds occurred at a level 2-1/2 feet above the clay in the V-1 pit floor, and thus a foot above the natural top of this base clay. The burned floor of this house is from 6 to 9 inches below the top of the loess town surface (P-8) as it slants up under the gumbo to continue as the Platform. The south and west walls of the V-4 residence were outlined for 16 by 15 feet by single rows of posts set 10 to 15 inches apart. They cut through a V-3b pit in Figure 31a. A hall or vestibule, 30" wide, extends outward 3 feet beyond the south wall at the SW corner.

The right angle of the lines of post molds of this V-4 building so directly parallels the wall trenches of the V-5 residence several inches above that they might have been mistaken for bench supports of the latter had V-4 not been completely sealed off beneath V-5's burned puddled clay floor.

The Latest Village Occupation, V-5
(Figs. 31, 32a, b; 33)

In the northeast excavation, the uppermost in the series of occupied village levels is extremely significant in that two structures, joined by a common burned ground surface (Fig. 32), constitute a commmunity complex of the usual rectangular full-Mississippian residence and a circular ceremonial house, both constructed on the same architectural principles.

It is in this fifth, and last, occupied Village level that a number of typical Middle Mississippian architectural features appear: wall trenches, prepared puddled clay floors and circular, hard-burned puddled clay fire basins with raised rim. Except for the trenches, these features were all found separately or in combination in the later occupation levels of the Platform sequence. The wall posts of both V-5 structures were 2-1/2 to 3 inches in diameter and were driven into the base of trenches, which were then filled with clay.

Circular Structure with Sub-surface Floor, V-5,
(Figs. 31b, background; 32a, b; 33a, b)

This structure was perfectly circular, 16-1/2 feet in diameter on the inside, with a sub-surface floor 10 inches below the level at which the wall trenches of both V-5 buildings appeared in a continuous burned ground surface. Apparently the wall trench and floor were dug separately (Fig. 32b), the floor having been dug first. A 4-inch wide molding, or curb, of the same puddled clay as lined the floor and fire pit was spread and smoothed against the 10-inch high sides of the circular excavation, slightly rounding to the ground surface and curving into the 3/8-inch layer of clay lining the floor. Then the wall trench could be dug beside the reinforced curb. It was one foot wide, 16-1/2 inches deep and went to the basal clay. The 2-1/2 inch thick

Fig. 31. Upper Village Occupation Levels in Northeast Excavation. Upper—Weekend volunteer finds shell disc bead in pit fill of V3b. Singly set posts of V4 house cut through pit, Vesibule. Arrow marks door of V5 wall-trenched residence. Platform slope to town surface p. 8 from rear. Lower—Final view of Northeast Excavation on December 14, 1941. Same corners of V4 and V5 houses in foreground. Temple Mound facet in left rear.

Fig. 32. Circular Ceremonial Structure associated with V5 Residence. Note matting covering outer wall and burned ground surface connecting the V5 structures that burned at the same time. Outer ring of supporting posts driven into base clay at rim of outer V1 pit. Upper—View from the southwest: Bones in Burial Apron are on pedestal. Lower—View from the southeast: Deep wall trench and puddled clay curb and floor.

wall posts were driven into the bottom of the trench and a mottled, yellowish clay was packed around them.

The fire pit, set 2 feet south of center, was 2-1/2 feet in diameter. Its rounded rim was 6 to 8 inches wide and was raised about 1-1/2 inch above the floor level; the rim and pit had been lined continuously with the puddled clay floor. Rather than a shallow, saucer-shaped basin as in the rectangular residences this is a *well* over 16 inches deep, with absolutely vertical sides and flat base. The intensity of firing of the clay walls and surrounding floor of this fire well indicates a continuous fire, or fires over a long period—another reason for regarding this structure as having a ceremonial function, besides the extra care in construction, the preservation of the old type of architecture in the sub-surface floor (compare with village level 1), and its circular shape which contrasts with the rectangularity of structures known to have been residences.

The wattle-and-daub walls of the circular structure were much thicker (at least at the base) than those of the rectangular structure—a foot wide as compared with 6 inches—and its wall trench was much deeper too. Its outer walls were covered with *mats* (Fig. 32a), the bottoms of which had been tucked into the outer side of the wall trench. Its roof was thatched with heavy layers of grasses. A large supporting post and a smaller one apparently braced a smokehole, on either side of it and dangerously close to the fire well, for they were charred below the heavily burned, puddled clay floor. Outside the thick wall another ring of larger posts, 3 inches in diameter, spaced at 2-1/2-foot intervals, had been driven or dug *straight* in about 1-1/2 feet deep. Thus one roof was not of the bee-hive type.

Rectangular Residence, V-5
(Figs. 31a and 32 arrow)

On this same burned ground surface, the rectangular house, whose north wall comes within 7 feet of the circular wall, has wall trenches only 6 inches wide at the corners and 4 inches along the sides. At one corner this trench is continuous and at the other broken. The posts, driven into a trench 9 inches deep (Fig. 30b, right 1/3 in riser of middle step), were placed much more closely together, at regular 6-inch intervals comparable with those of the P-4 house in the Submound Platform series. Dimensions are 19.6 feet (outside measurements) from north to south and over 21.5 feet from west to east (the east wall was not excavated). A charred roof beam was lying on the floor several feet inside the west wall and paralleling it, but no inner posts large enough to be considered primary roof supports were found.

The fire basin (Fig. 31a, after damaging in excavating V-4 beneath) was again slightly off center—only a foot to the south. It was 2-1/2 feet out of line, eastward, with the door in the south wall. This door is 9 feet from the southwest corner. The fire basin is smaller, shallower, and less deeply burned than either the fire well of the circular structure or the fire basin of the larger house on the P-4 level of the Platform. That this was used as a cooking fire is indicated by the presence of a smashed Ramey Incised pot about 15 inches in diameter with burned food residue on its inner surface. It was found on the burned floor quite near the fire basin, where it had been broken by the fall of the burning building, for burned wood and wattle and daub were strewn about it.

The uppermost occupation level in the village series is represented fragmentarily on the south side of the mound in the same square as the V-1 and V-3 levels. In this extension of the south excavation, V-5 is represented by an arc of four very small pole molds, 1 inch in diameter, with a hard outer-rim—probably cane. These may have been part of a meat-drying rack or door screen. These were at the same datum depth, 4 inches lower (-11.31'BD) on this south side, as a V-5 house whose burned floor was cut through by the Big Post pit more than 20 feet to the north.

The Submound Platform
(Figs. 30b, 31a, 33, 34, 35, 37)
Layer III

The close association of the final residence in the Village series with the ceremonial structure suggests that a clan head or priest may have lived there. The next series of five superimposed residences built on low platforms seems to confirm the inference that this area was occupied by an elite class. The individual platforms, raised and enlarged several times, were finally consolidated into a ceremonial Platform, 90 feet from north to south and 75 feet from east to west.

The occupation levels in the loess Platform are more significant for the number (6) of superimposed construction levels than for demonstrating new architectural developments.

The Platform was *built up piecemeal* both vertically and horizontally over an indefinite time period (Figs. 34, 35, 36).

The earliest platform house (P-3) stood only eight inches above the village surface (V-6) which covered another burned floor (V-5) in the SE excavation as well. These uppermost village levels had originally been designated P-1 and P-2—that's why P-3 actually starts the series of platform occupation levels. Four inches of weathered loess from the surrounding village area—the borrow pit still showing as a crescentic sag below the -9 foot contour line to the north and northeast of the residual mound (Fig. 43)—was added on top of P-3's low platform to make the more impressive P-4 residence

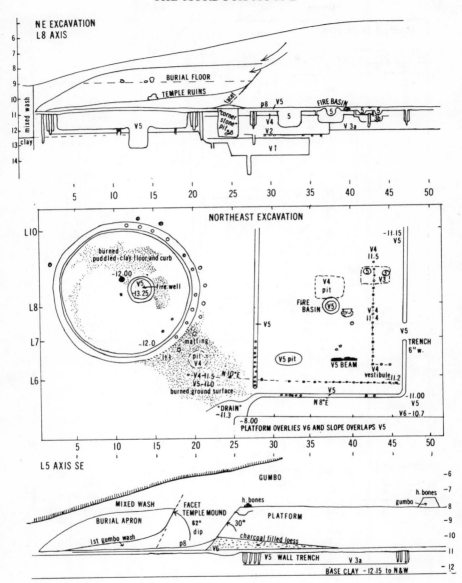

Fig. 33. Northeast Excavation: V5 ground plan with profile sections (exaggerated 2 times) N-S:L8 Axis through Circular Structure and Cornerstone Pit L5 Axis through Platform.

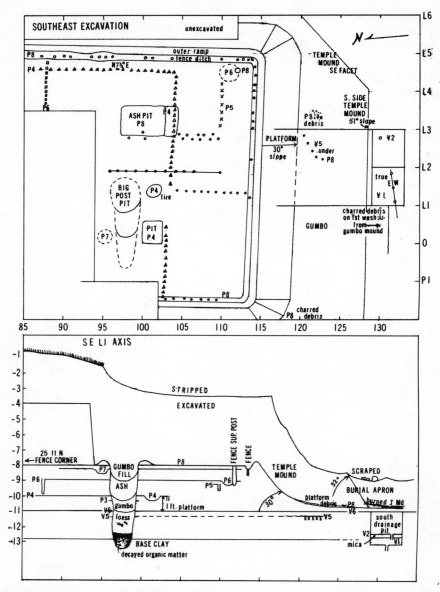

Fig. 34. Southeast Excavation: Ground Plan of Enclosure of SE quadrant of Platform. (Vertical section 2 times) N-S through middle of Enclosure L1 Axis.

stand a full foot above the ground. The platform of the next house (P-5) was 20 inches high, and P-6 stood a full 2 feet up on an individual platform some 50 feet wide, according to the position of its fire basin near the SE corner of the final Platform (Fig. 35, right foreground). This P-6 house platform was raised another six inches for the P-7 house and then 4 more inches added to reach the final height of 3 feet, in this quadrant of the Ceremonial Platform. The primary constituent of this SW quadrant was the P-6 and 7 house platform, which had to be trimmed at the east and south sides into 30° slopes oriented N 7°30′E and E 7°30′S. Sags midway in these east and south edges of the Platform, just beyond the fence, prove that a NE, SE, and apparently a SW quadrant were separate until this final stage. The Platform surface (P-8) can be followed (Fig. 31a) down the slope into a town level only a few inches above the village level (V-6).

The northeast quadrant rose in stages (Fig. 30b) contemporaneous with the elite houses of the Southeast quadrant. Profiles show a P-3 fire basin, a P-5 burned floor, and another P-6 floor again chopped off near its fire basin to form the northeast corner of the Platform.

The middle level house (P-4) was a large rectangular structure with a very wide doorway located on a foot-high platform, 20 inches below the final

Fig. 35. Enclosed area on Platform, showing underlying separate house platforms photo Monk's Mound in left background; Mound 51 to north in right rear.

Platform surface (P-8). Twenty-nine feet of its south wall and 17 of the east were excavated. If the wall posts of any of these platform houses were set in trenches, they didn't show in this less consolidated deposit. Most of the wall posts of the P-4 house are represented by holes rather than postmolds, the tops of which were sealed over by loess fill at the level of the burned P-4 house floor. This may be another example of the salvage and re-use of house posts. The posts were set only 6 inches apart, except for a 6 foot gap in the south wall beside the unusually large fire basin. Its rim was within 1.5 feet of a door post. This structure may be interpreted as a place for public functions to occur, as the large doorway would allow onlookers a view of the activities inside. Both Natchez and Illiniwek chiefs entertained many important visitors in their homes.

The top of the Platform measured 90 feet N-S by 75 feet E-W. Its worn, faceted corners (Figs. 30b, 35) and sloping sides dipped at a 30° angle from a still fairly well defined break at the top edges, as if the loess had been shaped and trampled from much use, possibly as a dance platform. The surface of the Platform was slightly undulating, reflecting the individual platforms that had eventually been consolidated into this single big one (Figs. 35, 36a).

The southeast quadrant was enclosed by a fence 48-1/2 feet long from south to north and 32 feet wide. The fence posts were the same size (2-1/2 to 3 inches in diameter) as the earlier house posts. They were set 16 inches deep and 9 inches to a foot or more apart into a shallow ditch 6 inches deep. Earth from the ditch had been piled outside the fence posts to form a foot-wide *crest* along this quadrant of the Platform. The crest raised the apparent height of this part of the Platform another 4 to 8 inches (Figs. 35, 36a).

The purpose of this enclosure could only have been to afford privacy for ceremonies centering on the Big Post erected in the middle of the southern half of it. Its base was set into the base clay at the deepest end of a sloping, extraction pit (Fig. 36b). Five feet east of the post was an enormous rectangular ash pit (Fig. 35, center).

The Murdock Surveyor

That both the Murdock Platform and Temple Mound and all the houses (after V-1 level) are oriented on a N-S axis (N 10-7°30′E) paralleling the sides of Monks Mound and the four others in this same row of subsidiary mounds, made it imperative that levels of features be carefully recorded.

It is so consistent an orientation as to foretell a city plan for at least the stockaded central area around Monks Mound, and one striking exception in the orientation of the Submound Platform conclusively ties in the time of the finishing of the Murdock Platform with the presence of Monks Mound, at least with the east side of its low southern terrace. The east side of the Murdock Platform as well as the east edge of the Monks Mound terrace are oriented

Fig. 36. Features of Enclosure. Upper—Fence posts (black squares) set in shallow ditch with crest piled at outside. Shallow end of Big Post Hole at right. Lower—Big Post Hole—post removed as final act on Platform since hole filled with the gumbo, composing overlying Temple Mound, over ash.

TABLE 2
MEASUREMENT IN RITUAL CONSTRUCTION
RECTANGULAR COORDINATES
Module: 16.5 feet = 5.03 meters

	North to South	East to West	Horizontal Diagonals (non-modular)
Circular Structure (V-5) (inside diameter)	16.5' (1x)		
Submound Platform:			
Base at V-6 surface	99' (6x) length	82.5' (5x) width	61x = 7.75+x
Platform top on P-8 surface	90.75' (5-1/2x)	74+ (4-1/2x)	
Enclosure:			
Fence exterior	49.5' (3x)	33' (2x)	13x = *ca.* 3-5/8x
Fence to Big Post	33'N (2x)	16.5' E (1x)	
	16.5' S (1x)	16.5' W (1x)	
Cornerstone pit at P-8 town surface	8.25' (1/2x) diameter		
Temple Mound			
Base at P-8 surface	115.5' (7x)	115.5'† (7x)[a]	98x = 9-7/8x
Temple Platform	66'* (4x)	44.375'† (2-3/4x)	23.56x
Terrace	90-3/4'† (5-1/2x)	33'† (2x)	34.25x
Proposed Initial Stage:			
Initial Base	99' (6x) Platform	99' (6x) Platform 16.5' East wing	72x = 8-1/2 (1.7" short)
Initial Terrace	75.5' (-x)	75.5' (-x)	11,400.5'

[a] Presumably, excavated to within 10 ft. of west lower face
* Estimated by geometric construction from excavated points
† Construction lines extended in accordance with erosion slopes
Direct measurements in **bold face**

identically at N7°30'E and the north and south sides of the Murdock Platform are placed at right angles to this orientation. But the west edge of the Platform is not on the orientation and diverges another 5° east, lengthening the south side of the Platform by a conspicuous 5 feet (Fig. 37).

The north baseline of the Platform was oriented at right angles (i.e. at E7°30'S) to the east baseline of the Platform, paralleling the south baseline 99 feet away. Measuring westward from an already constructed NE corner of the Platform, a pole must have been driven in at a distance of 82-1/2 feet to mark the NW corner. Then the west baseline for the Platform was lined up *optically*

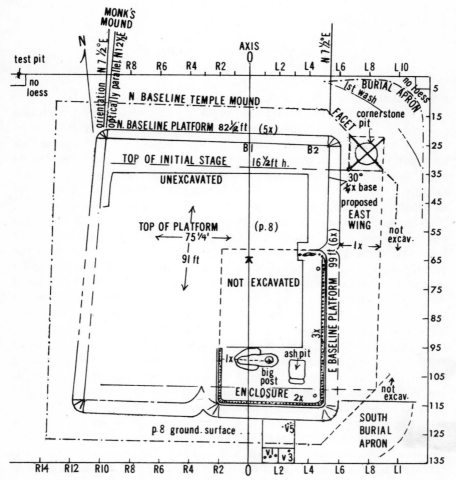

Fig. 37. Ground Plan of entire Platform, showing deviation of west baseline.

parallel with the east terrace face of Monks Mound, a block to the north and an avenue's width west. This must have been done by standing at various spots along the south edge of the Platform and sighting past the (necessary) pole at the NW corner until this line of sight seemed parallel rather than convergent (because of perspective), with the alignment of the east face of the big mound. This spot was actually 5 feet too far to the west, thus giving the Platform a west baseline oriented 5° further east of north rather than the standard orientation of all the other Murdock building lines and of the east terrace of Monks Mound itself (Fig. 37). This human error testifies to the presence of Monks Mound as the focal point of the Cahokia complex for some time prior to the building of the Murdock Temple Mound, for the latter's underlying Platform is worn from long use.

The Murdock Temple Mound
Layer IV

Reconstruction of the Temple Platform

If Murdock Temple Mound had proved to be the square-based, truncated pyramid its topographic map seemed to indicate, preservation in its stump of the original ground plan and angles of slope would not have enabled reconstruction of the height and dimensions of the temple platform. But its north face veered eastward, cutting diagonally across the area where I had thought I saw the NE corner outlined by bulging contour lines. A triangular face that I have named a "facet" joined the main north and east slopes.

Because of variant angles of slope in N-S and E-W profiles along the facet's diagonal baseline (from 56°N-S, Fig. 38b, to 66°E-W, at the left rear of Figs. 31b and 32b) I decided that a three-dimensional reconstruction of the mound might clarify the nature of the structure. By setting the profiles up on the ground plan and slicing down each angle of slope (Fig. 39b), I discovered that the NE facet had an angle of slope of 60°. Since the main faces had slopes of 52°, 51° and 50° (as measured by a Brunton compass— trigonometrically, this angle is 53°), the steeper plane of the facet could only have intersected the adjoining main faces up to a height of 33 feet. Truncated at this height, a rectangular platform 66 feet across (N-S) is delimited between the NE facet and an identical facet at the SE. A preliminary reconstruction in clay demonstrates this principle (Fig. 40a), but final dimensions were arrived at by more painstaking geometric construction.

Recognizing that the slope of a facet will always be steeper than that of the main faces, any faceted mound can be reconstructed by the two complimentary methods presented at the St. Louis Conference in 1966:

(1) *Geometrical* determination of the height of the mound and the dimensions of its temple platform, as described above.

Fig. 38. Faces of Temple Mound preserved and outlined by loess Burial Apron. Upper—At right is East Face on 42-1/2-foot Line at L 10 Axis (52°). Under root on left is the Facet corner at the 39-foot Line. Lower—N-S Profile on Left 6-1/2 Axis across face of Facet (56° slant here).

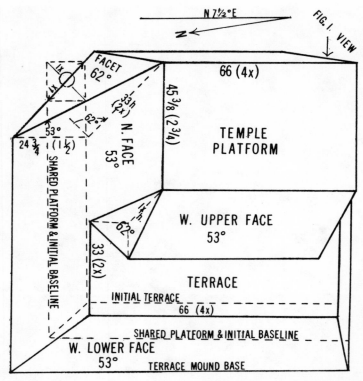

Fig. 39. Isometric reconstruction in Ritual Modules—16-1/2-foot units and quarter units.

(2) *Topographic* analysis of the differential surface wash, which reflects the form of the original earth structure.

Also because it was steeper, the NE facet of Murdock Mound gave way first, near its apex, undermining the temple platform at this corner. The surface wash down the face of the facet piled out in an alluvial fan beyond its baseline. This is known from excavation. Similarly the main slopes washed down, and outward from mid-face, to form a somewhat shallower scallop.

Superposition of the plan of Murdock Temple Mound on the contour map (1/2-foot contour lines were interpolated) shows a remarkable conformity of all construction lines with the residual slopes (Fig. 43). Thus Murdock Mound offers certain principles for analyzing differential wash, as it appears on a detailed topographic map of the eroded remnant of any (faceted) structure of hard-packed earth, in order to reconstruct its original form:
(1) Ground wash starts down the middle of each earth face, building back up that face in an alluvial fan and forming a *scallop* beyond its baseline.

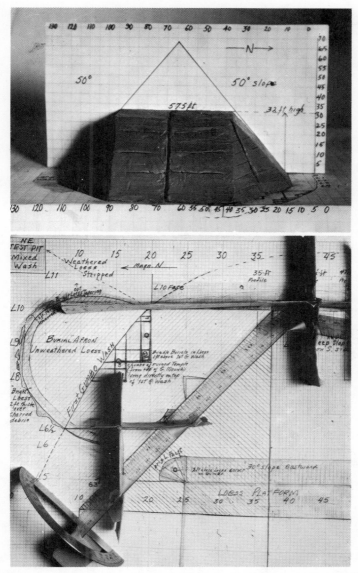

Fig. 40. Reconstructions of Murdock Temple Mound. Upper—In clay (1966): 1-foot short in height and 4-1/8 feet short at either side of temple platform. Lower—Reconstruction of facet slope from variant angles in profiles.

TABLE 3
MEASUREMENTS IN RITUAL CONSTRUCTION
TRIANGULAR COORDINATES

	Base	Height	Length of Slope	Angle	Formula
Faces: (The hypotenuses of vertical right triangles)					
Platform faces	**4-1/8'** (1/4x)	**2-1/2'**	**5-'**	**30°**	$\sqrt{3}$-1-2
Proposed Initial Terrace	11.7'	16-1/2' (1x)	20'	> 56°	
Temple Platform (N,S,E)	24-3/4'* (1-1/2x)	33'* (2x)	41-1/4'* (2-1/2x)	**53°**	3-4-5
Terrace, upper & lower (N,S,W)	12-3/8'* (3/4x)	16-1/2'† (1x)	20-3/4' (1-1/4x)	53°	3-4-5
Facets: (Resulting from diagonal joining of faces)					
Proposed Initial facets (NE baseline 16-1/2'* = 1x)	8-1/4'* (1/2x)	16-1/2' (1x)	19'	63-1/2°	
Temple Platform, NE & SE	**17-1/2'***	33'* (2x)	37-1/2'	**62°**	
Terrace, upper (N,S,W)	8-3/4'	16-1/2'† (1x)	18-3/4'	62°†	

Key:
* By geometric construction from excavated points
† Construction lines extended in accordance with erosion slopes
Figures in **bold face** measured directly

(2) The line of intersection of adjoining faces is held back, appearing as a smooth *notch* down the contour pattern from each platform corner.

Murdock Mound hints at a third principle, which is confirmed in the erosion of Monks Mound:

(3) In time, secondary erosion results in irregular gullies. They may interrupt a face and its basal scallop, but they are distinguishable from the even, and evenly spaced, notches that delimit each face.

It seems to be a combination of this diagnostic contour pattern of alternately scalloped and notched surface wash that has just led Coe (1968) to interpret a recent topographic map of the Great Pyramid at LaVenta, Vera Cruz, as a "fluted cone." I feel sure that its rectilinear platform, scalloped "corners" and sides, all separated by smooth notches, indicate that it was originally a faceted quadrilateral. A number of the Cahokia mounds [Moorehead (1928) described No. 65 as a cone too, despite its square platform] can be seen, on the map, (Fig. 13) to conform with the Olmecs' three-thousand-year-old prototype for all earth architecture in the Americas. I hope to give visual proof of this fundamental point in a paper I am preparing on Mesoamerican influences on the (Middle) Mississippi Culture.

Period of Construction

There were two indications that the Temple Mound was built rapidly, in contrast with the piecemeal consolidation of the Platform beneath it. First, no stratigraphic stages were discernible, and if my hypothesis of a 16-1/2-foot high stage is correct there would have been no floors above the platform within the 10.7-foot high remnant of the Temple Mound. Since the graves would then have been dug to a 7-foot depth from such a Terrace stage, I think it more likely they were shallow intrusions as the loading progressed.

Second, is the typological consistency of all potsherds (classified in the field as wares of the Monks Mound Aspect) throughout the temple mound fill with wares directly traceable to the final surface of the temple platform. In 1942 I surmised that, since wares in the fill came from some nearby site earlier than the time construction was started on the temple mound, "There must be some time difference within the Monks Mound Aspect." Wray, in 1952, seemed to have much the same impression: "The Trappist Focus, Late Mississippi, accounts for most of the remains at the Cahokia site ... It develops out of Old Village (Focus) and the distinction between the two is an arbitrary one " (Wray, 1952:160).

The youngest Murdock potsherds, along with charred debris from the temple platform, had been trapped on the tapered gumbo wash at the south side of the temple mound under a burial apron, just as had the chunks of temple wall with which they share A.D. 1370 as an end date for the completion and use of the temple. When did the project begin? If the Murdock

V-2 level correlates with the Eveland cross-shaped house at A.D. 1000 we have a total of 370 years at the Murdock site from the first hint of Mississippian developments here to the temple at the apex of Cahokia civilization. We can't just say that the Platform was finished any time after 1020 and the Temple Mound started any time after that.

The concept of the facet would also, at first thought, seem to demand rapid construction—a single stage execution based on a pre-existent plan for triangled corners to rise along with less steeply sloping sides to the 33-foot height at which they formed a rectangular platform on which to build the temple. However, the clay capped pit, which I considered as a part of the inaugural ceremonies, was off-center on the facet baseline. I also began to wonder how a pit, soon to be covered by gumbo wash, could mark the facet line for the substructure of a temple that wasn't completed until 1370—perhaps a hundred years later (assuming that the influence for temple building was out of Mexico in the religious fervor of the 1200's).

Hypothetical Initial or Terrace Stage

I then began to see the possibility that the Temple Mound had had an initial stage raised half the final height above the Platform's ground surface. Its purpose would have been to establish a square-based Terrace Stage, smaller but conforming with the square proportions of the final mound and with the terraced appearance of the western part of the topographic map (Fig. 43).

Keeping the longer dimension of the Platform base (99 ft, N-S) this would require the addition of 16-1/2 feet to the E-W dimension of the Platform (82-1/2 feet). Because the plaza was on the west, it had best be added entirely on the east side—an East Wing, as it were. (That may have been the original purpose, but mine was to see whether I could get that cornerstone pit to mark the middle of an *initial* facet).   Working backward (Fig. 41) the Temple Mound can be reconstructed in the following steps:

First. We extend the north baseline of the Platform eastward (maintaining its 7°30'S of E orientation) to its intersection with the facet line.

Second. Measure to the center of the pit cap (it measures 8-1/4 feet) and extend this same measurement an equal distance beyond the center of the pit along the facet line. This 16-1/2-foot facet line measures out at the new baseline of that East Wing, which itself is 16-1/2 feet east of the baseline of that East Wing, which itself is 16-1/2 feet east of the baseline of the Platform. Our intermediate stage base is now 99 feet square, with a smaller facet that foreordains a platform about half the final height of the temple platform.

Third. Extend the square inward from this 16-1/2 foot diagonal and we get 11-5/8 foot bases on which to slope up Initial North and East Faces and an 8-1/2 foot base for the Initial facet face—but how high? Try exactly half of the 33 foot height at which my reconstruction has placed the temple. The

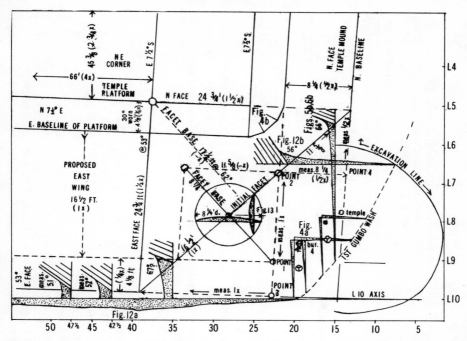

Fig. 41. Survey for Construction of Temple Mound in Two Stages. Detailed ground plan of northeast "corner."

resultant angle of slope for Initial faces is 56+° and for the Initial facet is 63° at a 16-1/2 foot height. These 16-1/2 foot dimensions must be more than redundant and will be looked into further.

To visualize this better, let's retrace this survey as the Murdock engineer may have done it. First, he measured the difference between the east and north baselines of the Platform: 99 feet minus 82-1/2 feet = 16-1/2 feet. He then laid out this measured distance east, and parallel to the old Platform baseline. Then both north and south baselines of the Platform were extended eastward to intersect the new eastern baseline. From the NE intersection survey point one might swing an arc inward, 1/2 unit in radius 8-1/4 feet and draw tangent to this arc the 16-1/2 foot diagonal facet baseline. The center of the baseline marks the center of the pit, one-half unit in diameter. The pit would then be dug and the thigh bone and quartz snake head placed in it, and capped with clay (as the Winnebagos used to cap important pits). Finally, the gumbo would be piled inward, soon obscuring the surveyed lines. This process would be repeated for the SE initial facet, which we know existed as a final facet because of the Burial Apron in the same location (Fig. 28).

TABLE 4
MEASUREMENTS IN RITUAL CONSTRUCTION
COMPOSITE DIMENSIONS OF RECTANGULAR AND TRIANGULAR COORDINATES

	Base of Face	Platform	Angle Base of Face	Total of Measurements
Platform:				
Ground Plan, N-S	**4-1/8'** (1/4x)	**90-3/4'** (5-1/2x)	—	**99'** (6x)
E-W	**4-1/8'** (1/4x)	**74-1/4'** (4-1/2x)	—	**82-1/2'** (5x)
Skyline Slope	**<5'** (< x)	N-S & E-W same as above	30°	—
Temple Mound:				
Proposed Initial §	11.7' (< x)	75.5' N-S & E-W (< x)	—	99' (6x)
Skyline Slope	20'	same as above	63-1/2°	—
Final Temple Mound:				
Ground Plan,				
East half (N-S)	24-3/4' * (1-1/2x)	66'* (4x), Temple platform	24-3/4'* (1-1/2x)	**115-1/2'** (7x)
West half (N-S)	12-3/8'† (3/4x)	90-3/4'† (5-1/2x), Terrace	12-3/8'† (3/4x)	**115-1/2'** (7x)
(E-W)	24-3/4'* (1-1/2x)	45-3/8'† (2-3/4x), Temple platform [+33'† (2x) or upper face 12-3/8'† (3/4x) + across terrace 20-5/8'† 1(1-1/4x)]	12-3/8'† (3/4x)	115-1/2'* (7x)
Skyline,				
East half (N-S)	**41-1/4'*** (2-1/2x)	66'* (4x), Temple platform	**53°**	—
West half (N-S)	20-3/8'† (1-1/4x)	90-3/4'† (5-1/2x), Terrace	20-3/8'† (1-1/4x)	—
(E-W)	41-1/4'* (2-1/2x)	45-3/8'† (2-3/4x), Temple platform 20-5/8'† (1-1/4x) upper west face 20-5/8'† (1-1/4x) across terrace 20-5/8'† (1-1/4x) lower west face	12-3/8'† (3/4x)	—

§ by construction to 16-1/2'
facet baseline and height (1x)

Key: * By geometric construction from excavated points
† Construction lines extended in accordance with erosion slopes
Figures in **bold face** measured directly

The Ritual Module

The 16-1/2 foot module of Murdock Mound takes on more credence when considered in the light of the 57 meter module recognized in the city planning at Teotihuacan (Millon, 1967). James Marshall, a civil engineer, has pointed out to me (personal communication) that a 66-foot measurement he had noted several times in his triangulated survey of the earthworks at Newark, Ohio, equals one fourth the diagonal of the Teotihuacan 57-meter module. That Marshall was on the track of not only a midwestern module but of a derivation from Mexico is verified by the fact that the 16-1/2 foot Murdock unit equals one fourth of 66 feet.

However, none of the residential structures beneath Murdock Mound conform to the 16-1/2 foot unit (or fraction of it), and the sides and diagonals of houses at Hiawassee Island (as measured by Marshall) do not correlate either. The module (16-1/2 feet) then, was apparently used only in conjunction with ritual construction. Everything with a ritual content at Murdock Mound does divide exactly into 16-1/2 foot multiples or quarters. All of the measurements used in ritual structures at Murdock Mound are listed in Table 5.

Until now, published dimensions of Mexican structures have been contradictory and my module correlations from small-scale ground plans inconclusive. In Stierlin's (1968) book on ancient Mexican architecture, photographs show that rubble has now been cleared from most of the baselines, and Stierlin gives measurements of 42 buildings to the nearest .1 foot. These prove that pre-Columbian architecture at twelve Mexican sites, from Olmecs to Aztecs, was based on the 16-1/2-foot module. Of Stierlin's 121 measurements, 74 divide exactly into 16.5 foot units and 39 into *fifths* of that unit (3.3 feet). Two are half-modules, both at Mitla, where fifths also appear four times. Only six of of the 121 dimensions are non-modular. It's regrettable that I can find no evidence for a Mexican super-unit of 66 feet, since the Mexican fractional measure of 1/5x, used from LaVenta on, would thereby correspond even better with their vigesimal system of mathematics. The quarter-module subdivisions discovered at Murdock could well have been a provincial adaptation—concomitant with using half-scale elevations of the 3-4-5 triangle. I have not yet plotted the angles of slope of Mexican structures from these new dimensions to determine their triangle formulae.

Completion of the Murdock Temple Mound

The 16-1/2 foot unit needed to expand the Platform's 6x north-south dimension to the 7x required for the Temple Mound's base was added, as 1/2x (8-1/4 feet) built out from both north and south baselines of the Platform. Then why were the engineers' additions to the east (and unexcavated west, I presume) so unequally divided? Oddly confirmatory both of these

TABLE 5

CONVERSION TABLE TO RITUAL MODULE

Ritual Module:	Feet:	Meters:
1/4x	4.28	1.26
1/2x	8.25	2.52
3/4x	12.37	3.78
1x	16.50	5.03
2x	33.00	10.06
3x	49.50	15.09
4x	66.00	20.12
5x	82.50	25.12
6x	99.00	30.18
7x	115.50	35.21
8x	132.00	40.24
9x	148.50	45.27
10x	165.00	50.30
11x	181.00	55.33
12x	198.00	60.36

having been an initial, or Terrace, stage of Murdock Mound, and of the professional caliber of its architects and engineers are the very specific proportions that were added as shown in the detail of the NE "corner" (Fig. 41). Here the baseline and angles of slope of the Platform, Temple Mound and final facet were found in the ground, while the dotted lines are my own constructions.

The Murdock surveyor may have extended his Platform baseline yet further eastward, just as I had, and stood at Point 2—the northwest corner of his initial stage facet which would have remained a definite point of intersection after the cornerstone pit was hidden by wash. From here he measured off one module along the oriented E-W line and marked Point 3. Standing here he would have swung his measuring rod to intersect the facet line he had extended to the southeast. This established the amount the Temple Mound base was to be expanded eastward, 4-1/8 feet from the Initial east baseline. The new facet corner, at my 39-foot line, delimited the northern end of the east face, and concomitantly, of the temple platform.　　Besides these horizontal dimensions, the angle and length of slope of the east face were also predetermined by the location of this strategic facet corner, which shows as a hump at Line 39 on the profile of the L10 Axis of Figure 41. Notice how the tapered wash recedes from it in *both* directions—diminishing rapidly to the north as the facet drops back abruptly to the northwest, and lowering gradually to the south as the east base line diverges by 2°30′ (N7°30′E minus

5° for magnetic north) from the excavation line. The photo (Fig. 38a) shows this same intersection of the NE facet with the East face at the 39 foot line in the middle left, and the East face itself to the right. My field measurement of the dip of this face, was 52° and on other main faces the reading was 50 and 51. The trigonometrically correct angle was 53° however.

The ultimate purpose of the engineer in adding 1-1/4x of the total 2x E-W expansion on this east side was to get a base-of-face twice as wide (24-3/4 feet or 1-1/2x) and thereby twice the height (33 feet) for this half on which the temple would stand as was needed for the 1x high Terrace on the west.

Rectangular or Triangular Coordinates at Cahokia?

The answer in Murdock Mound is both, because the triangle formula used by the Murdock architect automatically established module dimensions on all planes. They are in the ratio of 3 times 1/2x on ground plans to 4 times 1/2x on elevations, giving 5 times 1/2x dimensions on slopes. That the angle of slope to the ground in this right triangle construction happened to be 53° was, I believe, irrelevant and unknown to the builders of the mound.

Regardless of whether the Murdock architect's aim was to achieve a specific elevation or a length of slope, expressed in module units, his combinations of *bases* were related in rectangular coordinates on which they too were expressed in modules. The architect of the surveyed ground plan had proportioned a 7x square base into multiple modules and quarter modules along rectangular coordinates. He used these proportions as the bases of vertical triangles lined up with the ground plans of the upper levels. These baselines were designed as the means of achieving a *skyline* whose slopes balanced platforms (Figs. 42a, b).

The Murdock module, first spotted on hypothetical triangles, would not have checked out in rectangular coordinates on ground plans had the 3-4-5 triangle formula not been used. This is fundamentally a triangulation system, and it has been pointed out that the Murdock module relates to the diagonal correlate (on a 45° triangle) of the 57 meter module recorded for rectangular coordinates by modern archaeologists in Mexico.

So, as far as I can see, Cahokia engineers dealt only with right triangles, and the formula for Murdock Temple Mound was based only on vertical elevations of the right triangle proportioned 3-4-5 (The Platform slope is a 30°-60° triangle but may have been constructed pragmatically on a 1/4x base). Having decided on a final temple platform 2 modules high (or 4 half-modules), bases 1-1/2 modules (3 half-modules) long were measured off to intersect at right angles on the ground plan. The slope of the main face would be completed when earth had been piled up inside the baseline on a slant that must measure 2-1/2x (5 half-modules) when it had reached the specified total

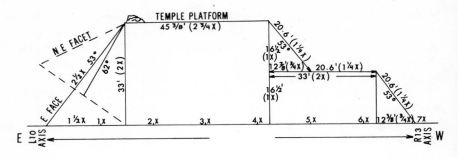

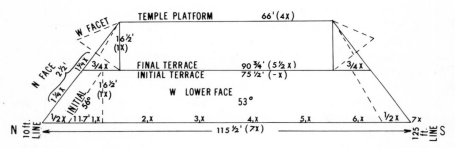

Fig. 42. Cross sections of Murdock Mound in modules (no vertical ex-
aggeration): (a) From East (left) to West (right) as seen from Monk's Mound;
(b) From North (left) to South (right) as seen from Plaza.

2x height. If there had been an initial stage, length of slope would have to be
the determinative factor because a stepped baseline would be hard to measure
or to measure up from. Then the height of the earth loading was kept level up
to the same dimension for the base of the face measured inward from the
opposite baseline. From there the earth loading was slanted back down to that
opposite baseline.

In practice then the facet was an *architectural* feature and did not
predetermine any of the dimensions specified by formula in module measurements. Rather it was the resultant of these specifications, the dirt simply
being piled up diagonally out to the facet baseline from inside the wedge left
between adjoining main faces. Naturally, the apex of this triangular face was
built to meet the main faces at the corner of the temple platform, whose
height and dimensions had already been *established* by the planning and construction of the adjoining main faces. The same applies to the 1x high facet
with corresponding half dimensions that I think shows in scalloped contour

lines (Fig. 43) at either end of the upper west face leading up from the
terrace to the temple platform.

The Murdock architect dealt consciously with harmonious proportions
and applied principles of good design, especially adapting them to the material
in which they would be executed. The facet was the aesthetic invention of
architects designing for construction in *earth*. I can't think of any parallel in
stone or mud brick. The facet was a device for cutting down the squatty
appearance inherent in earth construction and producing the most impressive
setting possible for the temple. It stopped the eye directly behind the base of
the temple, so that this crowning structure seemed more towering without a
long diminuendo stretching back behind it. The minor side facets from terrace
to platform led the eye up a more vertical-seeming panel made to look the
same width as the temple platform. The combination of squared front terrace
and high, faceted rear presented a more imposing facade that was intensified

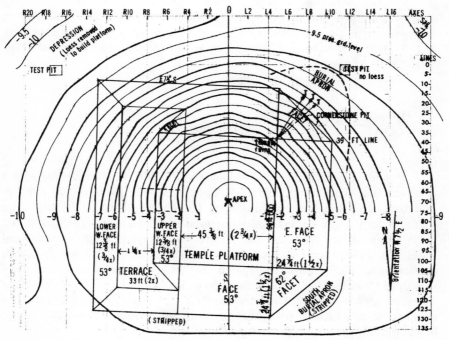

Fig. 43. Pre-excavation Contour Map (made to 1-foot intervals with 1/2-foot
lines interpolated) superimposed on Ground Plan of Murdock Temple Mound,
shaded for slopes. Wide-spaced shading on excavated areas and their extension.

by an effect of forced perspective to the rear. This pattern was designed to make earth architecture as impressive as possible. That the facet also made it stronger (serving as a corner brace) may not have been intentional.

The Temple Structure

Whether the Murdock Temple Mound rose as a continuous operation or in stages, you will recall that its final platform has finally been reconstructed to a 33 foot height and with the dimensions 66 feet (4x) by 45-3/8 feet (2-3/4x). The temple built on this platform had very thick walls of wattle and daub. This temple must have been built almost to the edge of its platform, at least at the NE corner.

The temple burned at the time the mound was abandoned. The compacted slopes of the sub-structure held up for an indefinite time. Since its completion only a thin mud wash had run down the faces after every rain and rounded out in a tapering black redeposit beyond its baselines. Then the weakest spot gave way—the facet, whose 62° dip was more unstable than the 53° main faces. The corner of the temple platform washed out at the apex of the facet, undermining the temple ruins at this northeast corner. Four big chunks of burned temple wall went tumbling down the facet, and came to rest, sunk about a half inch into the top of the tapered first gumbo wash (Fig. 41, "T"s). It is the charcoal picked out of this temple debris that was dated A.D. 1370± 20 years.

Artifacts

Pottery

It was recognized through field observation that we were dealing with a developmental sequence of Middle Mississippi pottery wares out of a Woodland base. This had been confirmed by Dr. Thorne Deuel in the field. The Village pottery sequence was from grit-tempered, cord-marked grey ware found on the floor of the V-1 house (*not* washed in) through a variety of red-filmed wares that I called grit-tempered in my field notes. Some of these proved to be limestone and/or pottery-tempered. In direct association with the fully developed Middle Mississippi architectural levels were the fully developed wares, all shell-tempered. These included red and black polished types, and a complete Ramey-Incised, flare-shouldered pot (with burned stew in it) found beside the fire basin of a V-5 wall-trenched house.

Unfortunately, a typological study had been begun on these materials which were stored at the Illinois State Museum without first noting the provenience on the sherds; thus no statistical data is available on this pottery.

Torch Holder (?): Also to be mentioned under pottery is a crude, pear-shaped blob of clay some seven inches in diameter and about the same height. A vertical hole, about an inch across, made me think it might have been a torch holder. It seemed more likely burned during a conflagration than intentionally fired.

Stone Artifacts

Three small triangular white flint points were found on the P-8 surface, under the gumbo, along with some red-slipped, shell-tempered potsherds, at the base of the ceremonial Platform (P-8). The points could have dropped back to the foot of the fence during a skirmish (Fig. 34, vertical).

In addition was a pale yellow quartz pebble about an inch and a quarter long which had been reworked by pecking. It was formed into a snake head—a pit viper (strongly resembling Mexican portrayals of the rattlesnake), having wide-spaced eyes, everted lips, a scaley flattened head, and spread jaws. It was found associated with a human thigh bone in a clay-capped pit which had been dug from the final P-8 ground surface to mark the diagonal corner ("facet") up to which the Temple Mound was to be built.

Shell

One shell disc bead had been swept into the ash fill of a V-3 house pit (Fig. 31a).

The absence of artifacts in or around the pits indicated to us that there may have been a separate specific area in which rubbish materials were dumped. Recently I've learned of the excavation of Mound 51 by Charles Bareis of the University of Illinois (personal communication) in which a dump was uncovered. This mound is located less than a block north of Murdock Mound, in the same North-South line of mounds.

Burials

Human skeletal remains were designated as "Bundle Burials" (nos. 1-12) and were interred three separate times during the period of the Temple Mound: (A) immediately before construction, (B) during construction building, and (C) shortly after abandonment.

The treatment of these dead showed the disregard that might have been accorded sacrificial victims (possibly victims of cannibalism); moreover, that they had been placed in spots of sacred context also may indicate they were offerings.

A. Human remains on P-8 surface at the *inauguration* of the temple mound-building program:

The only association of an artifact with any of the human bones was the little quartz snake head in the "cornerstone" pit (Fig. 39a) along with a human femur, designated "Bundle Burial No. 3." Deposited at the same time were two little heaps of human bones without skulls along the north edge of the ceremonial Platform. Whether this was just a convenient surface on which to get rid of some bones, since they were to be covered immediately with gumbo, or whether this was another observance connected with inauguration of the construction of the mound can only be decided if parallel examples are reported from other Mississippi sites.

B. Human remains *in* the temple Mound:

Another small pile of human bones was found in the gumbo only a foot above the east edge of the loess Platform. The other four fragmentary "burials" (one including deer bone as well) were all in (now) shallow pits filled with lighter soil. No ground surface on the gumbo from which these had been dug was detectable and bases of the pits came within a foot of the present ground surface in a ten-foot wide strip stretching eastward from the present apex. One was five and one-half feet and the three others between seven and eight feet above the underlying Platform, but they don't seem to be layers representing separate building stages of the gumbo mound. Rather, they conform with the curve of the eroded surface.

C. *Burial Aprons*—after abandonment of the Temple:

Five more piles of human bones, two including skulls, were placed on a prepared floor a foot high in the Northeast Burial Apron. The lower jaw of one of these had been dropped on the burial floor about five feet away from the skull it seemed to match, which was placed on long bones and ribs that might have belonged to a single individual. The number of skeletons that had been stripped from the Southeast apron (Fig. 28) is not known.

The nature of these "burials" may possibly be explained by recent suggestions of the presence of cannibalism at Cahokia.

Summary

The area where the V-1 pit house was dug remained a depression, a ready-made saucer pit, attractive to the next resident. I suggest that both of the V-3 levels and V-4 were in an established Early Mississippi village with an expanding population. From whatever time they started building Monks Mound, Lot 22, less than a block away, would have been a very desirable location.

The association of the religious (and/or clan) structure with a "better class" residence on the V-5 level is a clue to Lot 22's being already in a prestige neighborhood, and the following succession of large houses on low platforms adds substance to this theory that Cahokia at the town stage had its elite social class. The P-4 house, on its foot-high platform, was definitely the biggest and best, and may even be called a "chief's" house.

I am confident that at least the east face of the terrace of Monks Mound existed in its present form when the final consolidation of the Murdock Platform was lined up with it, by optical illusion. How long the Murdock Platform persisted in whatever was the ceremonial function of its Big Post enclosure can only be estimated from its hard—packed (dance?) floor, both within and around the enclosure, and by the rounding from wear of all its originally angular edges and facets. The amount of ash alone tells of many roaring fires in the enclosure before the final celebration, after which the Big Post was salvaged and its bathtub pit half filled with ash. This was the inaugural ceremony for the erection of the Temple Mound, and I think the digging of the cornerstone pit and the deposition of human bones on the opposite (NE) edge of the Platform were all parts of the same ceremonial observance. Loads of gumbo for the temple mound were then brought in.

It seems however, that they used some loess just at first, piling it alternately with basket-loads of gumbo and yellow clay on top of the bones along the north edge of the Platform to a height of 4 feet, by vertical loading. The north face seems the logical place for work to have begun in relation to the adjoining "survey corner." On the southeast enclosure pure gumbo was thrown into the Big Post hole (Fig. 36b) and piled right on up to at least the 1941 apex of the mound, and presumably to its completed height of 33 feet. The fine mud that washed down the sides of the mound to form that tapering margin around its base is as black as coal, even when dry, and Murdock Temple Mound must have looked quite handsome when completed.

And it made an impressive ruin too, with the red-burned clay from the temple walls streaking its black sides—impressive enough to continue (or soon resume) being a sacred place after it ceased being an active place of worship.

The black slopes still stood firm (except where the facet was gullied down its middle and some chunks of temple wall came tumbling down the gully) when what I have called "Burial" Aprons were piled against their base, thus fortunately preserving the stump of the temple mound from erosion. It could have been the same generation of Cahokians that saw the temple burn (or the next) who brought the bright unweathered loess from the Collinsville Bluffs to prepare a place to dispose of, or offer, human remains. It is the unceremonious treatment no people would have given their own dead that inclines me to think it was Cahokians putting strangers there (following the observances of their forefathers, as in the inaugural ceremonies for building Murdock Mound), rather than strangers that had taken over after the hypothetical fall of the city, who made this final human entry in the record contained in the Murdock Mound site.

References Cited

Coe, Michael D.

    1968 *America's First Civilization (Discovering the Olmec)*, American Heritage Publishing Company, Inc., in association with the Smithsonian Institution. Distributed by D. Van Nostrand Company, Inc. pp. 53, 56, 64.

Millon, René

    1967 Teotihuacan. *Scientific American.* Vol. 216 (No. 6), pp. 38-48. New York.

Moorehead, Warren K.

    1928 The Cahokia Mounds. *University of Illinois Bulletin 26.* No. 4. Urbana.

Smith, Harriet M.

    1942 Preliminary Report. *Journal of Illinois State Archaeological Society.* Vol. 1 (No. 1).

    1963 *Prehistoric People of Illinois.* Museum Storybook. Field Museum of Chicago.

Stierlin, Henri

    1968 *Living Architecture: Ancient Mexican.* Grosset & Dunlap, New York.

Walker, Winslow M., and Robert McCormick Adams

    1946 *Excavations in the Matthews Site, New Madrid County, Missouri. Transactions of the Academy of Science of St. Louis.* Vol. 31 (No. 4), pp. 75-120. St. Louis.

Wray, Donald E.

    1952 "Archaeology of the Illinois Valley" in *Archeology of Eastern United States,* ed. James B. Griffin. University of Chicago Press, Chicago.

A CAHOKIA PALISADE SEQUENCE

James Anderson
University of Wisconsin-Milwaukee
Milwaukee, Wisc.

Based on his work at Aztalan and an early description of Cahokia by Brackenridge, S.A. Barrett wrote in 1933: "Certainly we would feel no surprise if lines of postmolds delineating stockades were eventually found here at Cahokia." (Barrett, 1933:60). About this same time Dache Reeves (Col. U.S.A.F. Ret.) took aerial photographs of Cahokia which would eventually prove Barrett correct.

Thirty-three years later the University of Wisconsin-Milwaukee Cahokia Project headed by M.L. Fowler discovered evidence of stockades at Cahokia. The stockades were identified first from the Reeves photographs by Fowler, Charles J. Bareis and Nelson Reed. Several white lines on the photographs formed a pattern around the central group of mounds which was not consistent with other patterns of white streaks representing channel changes of the Mississippi River, Cahokia and Canteen Creeks and other natural erosion (Fig. 44). These aberrant white lines were thought to represent soil disturbance caused by the construction of a prehistoric wall. The lines were also later identified on earlier oblique photographs taken in 1922 (Hall, 1968: 75-78). Continued cultivation and deep plowing techniques have tended to make the lines less clear although still visible on photographs taken in the 40's, 50's and 60's.

The funds for this project were supplied by the National Science Foundation under the terms of two grants awarded to Fowler (GS1098 and GS2119). The University of Wisconsin-Milwaukee provided equipment and laboratory space. Permission to excavate in Cahokia Mounds State Park was granted by William T. Lodge, Director of the State of Illinois Department of Conservation. The author served as project assistant and supervised the stockade excavations in 1966 and 1967. Because of expanded duties, direct supervision of the 1968 stockade excavation was turned over to Wayne Glander, University of Wisconsin-Milwaukee graduate student.

The stockade line, approximately 200 meters east of Monks Mound was confirmed during the '66 and '67 field seasons. About 120 meters of stockade trenches were exposed in two large excavation units (A and B, Fig. 45). Wall trenches of the proper width were also exposed in test trenches near Highway 40 and on the edge of the slough (C and D, Fig. 45).

Fig. 44. Aerial Photograph of the Monks Mound area showing the white lines of the palisade disturbance to the east (right).

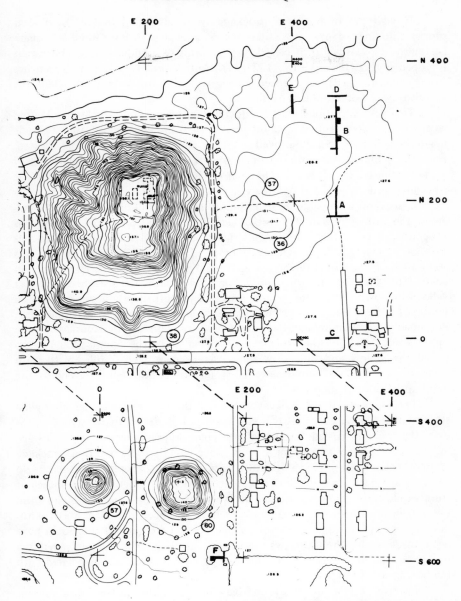

Fig. 45. The map of the central sections of the Cahokia Mound site showing
the various locations of palisade excavations conducted by the University of
Wisconsin-Milwaukee.

Three types of bastioned stockades were identified in unit B. A clear superpositioning of the stockades shows a change from round to square bastions with backwalls (or closed gorge) to square bastions with no backwalls (or open gorge) (Black, 1967: 122-123). Unit A produced four wall trenches (some superimposed), a screened entryway and possible bastions. Only the entryway was worked out in detail.

The '68 excavations were conducted 600 meters south of Monks Mound where it appeared from the photographs the southern end of the stockade might be (F, Fig. 45). Four wall trenches and three bastions were located. Here the building stages went from round to open gorge bastions, no closed gorge bastions were observed. The goal of this paper is to briefly describe the stockades in units B and F and the entryway.

Traces of a possible buried humus layer were found 80 to 100 cm. below the surface in unit B. Positive identification was prevented because this zone was so cut up by storage pits, house floors and the stockade trenches that only small sections remained intact. The soil above the humus was composed of the same finely textured sandy material and differed only in color. The first 20 cm. were brownish black and plow disturbed; the rest yellowish brown. Under the humus was an undisturbed yellow zone similar in texture to the deposit above the humus followed by undisturbed blue clay. Presumably the humus and the soils below were one of the sources for the upper zone. Many of the storage pits originated in the "humus" and penetrated the yellow and blue clay zones. As the pits were refilled with trash some of the backfill would have been left over thus contributing to the build-up of the top zone.

The stockade trenches were excavated through many earlier aboriginal storage pits and houses, mostly Late Woodland Bluff. In two instances however, the trenches passed through Mississippian houses. Ceramic and C-14 age estimates of the Mississippian houses place erection of the first stockade around A.D. 1100 (1135±85 GX0859, Geochron Laboratories Inc.). No accurate age data are available at present for the last stockade. No houses or storage pits were found to overlay the wall trenches. Two wood samples from posts associated with the third stockade have not been dated. A burial without offerings intruded into a closed gorge bastion trench, but this could have been made while the third wall was still standing. The lack of overlying occupational debris may indicate the open gorge stockade was associated with the last phase of Cahokia.

Feature 26 (Fig. 46) has round bastions and is the earliest in the present sequence. Approximately 66 meters of uninterrupted curtain or wall trench between bastions (Black, 1967: 122-123) and two bastions were excavated. This feature, as were features 27 and 28, was recognized anywhere from 10 to 20 cm. below the plow zone. Bastions have an inside diameter of 2.5 to 3.0

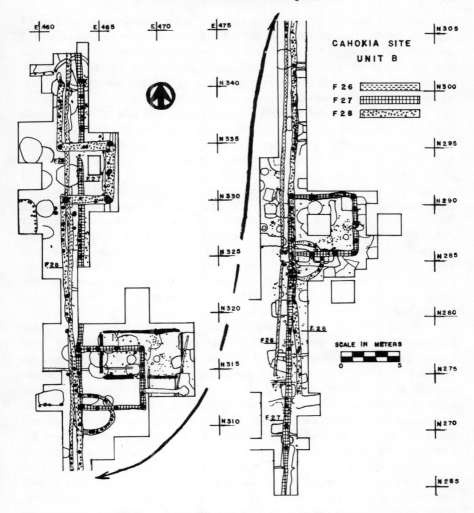

Fig. 46. A plan view of the palisade excavation showing the alignment of the palisade trenches and locations of the curtain trenches and bastions.

meters. Width of the bastion trenches at the top varies 40 to 45 cm. and from 30 to 35 at the bottom which is generally flat. Postmolds are round (15-20 cm.) in diameter and spaced from 10 to 60 cm. apart. Maximum inside distance between bastions is 20.5 meters.

The curtain trench of feature 26 had a flaring mouth, either straight or drastically tapering sidewalls and rounded floors. The trench measured 50 to

60 cm. at the mouth, 40 cm. below the flare and sometimes narrrowed to 14 cm. The few postmolds visible in the fill had the same diameters as those in the bastions. Floors of both were from 90 to 100 cm. below surface and were not penetrated by postmolds. The floor of the curtain was 10 to 20 cm. shallower behind the bastions perhaps indicating the absence of several uprights to permit entry into the tower.

Square, closed gorge bastions and postmolds extending below the trench floors, are the main characteristics of the second stockade, feature 27. The bastions enclose an area of about 4.8 meters square. Trenches are straight walled with a width of 40 cm. The floors of both bastion and curtain trenches are flat with rounded corners. Depths range from 1.6 to 1.8 meters below surface for both. It will be noted from the map (Fig. 46) that there are opposing pairs of postmolds in the bastions suggesting support posts for a floor or platform. The postmolds in the bastion average 40 cm. in diameter and were 60 to 80 cm. below the floor. In the curtain trench the major postmolds averaged 30 cm. in diameter, extended 40 cm. below the floor and were 1.5 to 2.0 meters apart. The small uprights were 15 to 20 cm. in diameter. Approximately 80 meters of feature 27 have been excavated. The trench was interrupted between N333.90 and the edge of the open gorge bastion and is a possible entryway.

Feature 28, the last stockade in this series, has square, open gorge bastions. This feature was regarded as a repair wall until late in the 1966 season when the wall diverged from feature 27 and passed over feature 26 between N315 and 325. A bastion was located in 1967 confirming its identification as a separate stockade. Only one bastion for this stockade was exposed but trenches with similar connections to the curtain trench suggest an interval of about 40 meters between bastions. Interestingly the bastion was located approximately where the third set of superimposed bastions was expected. The bastion is 4 meters across and was at one time completely rebuilt. The dotted line (Fig. 46) outlines a second bastion trench with small posts. Post molds extended below the floor about 80 cm. for the first and 60 cm. for the second. Diameters ranged from 40 cm. to 60 cm. for the first and 20 to 30 cm. for the second. Widths and profiles were similar varying from 50 to 60 cm. at the mouth and tapering to 40 cm. above the flat floor. The floor depth of the earliest bastion was 1.9 meters below surface or about 40 cm. deeper than the second.

In other construction details feature 28 was like feature 27. Widths and cross sections of the curtains compare favorably but the floor of feature 27 is 30 cm. deeper. Not as many large post molds were recorded for feature 28 because the posts extended into the fill of feature 27 and did not leave a very noticeable mold. About 80 meters of this stockade were excavated. The trench was traced to N341.30 where it turned slightly to the west and terminated. Excavation to the north and west produced several features including an east/west wall trench. A test (E, Fig. 45) midway between Monks Mound and unit B did not reveal a continuation of this trench and feature 28 may begin again north of the excavation limits.

The entryway in unit A (not illustrated) is about 90 meters south of unit B. The entryway resembles an open gorge bastion with one of the flanks or sides missing. The east and north sides were enclosed. The interior is rectangular and measures 6.5 meters east-west and 2.5 meters north-south. The trench was 40 to 50 cm. wide at the top, about 1.0 meter deep, fairly straight walled and had a flattened to rounded floor. Postmolds were rare and none were below floor level. There would be no need for heavy deep posts for supporting a platform in the entry. Without a positive link-up of the curtain trenches in units A and B the entryway cannot be associated with any of the three stockades.

The excavations south of Monks Mound were designed to once again test the details indicated on the Reeves photographs and to find a stockade unencumbered with other kinds of construction. The first objective was successful, the second only partly so. The land in this area is low and wet into late spring or early summer. It was never very suited to modern agriculture and was cultivated only in drought years. Previous testing 100 meters further south on another problem had indicated that the land was little used by the Indians. There was indeed a low incidence of disturbance directly attributable to residential occupation. Instead there were a number of meandering fill areas which changed in horizontal plan with every level.

The soil profile consisted of a dark humus plow zone 25 cm. deep, and 20 to 30 cm. thick disturbed brownish grey sandy clay mixture grading into a disturbed tan clay band 30 cm. deep, a thin cream colored clay zone of less than 5 cm., and a blue grey undisturbed clay. In 1968 as much as 1.0 meter of overburden had to be removed before reaching an acceptable level for recognition of cultural features.

The stockade trenches and bastions were uncovered in one excavation unit 10 by 20 meters (not illustrated). Three of the trenches came from the northeast as expected but one appeared to come from the southeast. Relating bastions and stockade trenches with certainty was not possible. The stockade trenches at the east end of the unit were widely spaced but in the area of the bastions braided even more than those east of Monks Mound.

The intersection of curtain and flank trenches should have occured in a one meter square block. Approaching the vicinity of the connections the four trenches blended into two pairs. One pair was erased 2 meters from the connection by a fill area. The trenches coming from the north are probably related to the round and open gorge bastions studied in the 1966 and 1967 excavations (Fig. 45, A and B). The trench appearing to turn from the south is unexplained.

Fig. 47. Excavation of the palisade trench showing the main curtain trench of the second palisade.

The round bastion is the earliest and a carbon of the ones previously described. Diameters were 3.2 meters inside and overall 4.0 meters. Postmolds were 20 to 30 cm. in diameter and spaced as close as 10 cm. and as far apart as 60 cm. Nineteen postmolds were counted in the trench. The shortened cross section (1.0-1.4 meters below the surface) suggests a trench with straight walls and flat to rounded floor.

All but 2 meters of the open gorge bastions were exposed. A large tree growing at the west intersection of the curtain and bastion trenches prevented complete exposure. The right flank or east side of the bastions cut the round bastion. In unit B it was the left flank or south side, of the closed gorge bastion which halved the round bastion. The first of the open gorge bastions imitates the 1967 example. The second does not, being longer than it is wide. The first is nearly square having an inside measurement of 3.60 meters. The trench walls slope in from 50 to 60 cm. at the level of recognition (80 cm. below the surface) to 30 cm., 10 cm. above the floor level. The floor appears more rounded than in feature 28 bastion and is 1.70 meters below surface. The oblong postmolds of the large support posts were 50 by 30 cm. and exceeded the bottom of the trench at least 30 cm. The intermediate post-molds averaged 20 to 25 cm. and bottomed at floor level.

The second bastion utilized the side trenches of the first but increased their length about two meters creating a bastion with an inside measurement of 3.8 by 5.4 meters. This bastion was identified at 80 cm. below surface. The floor sloped downward from 90 cm. below surface at the front to 1.20 meters below surface at the curtain connection, all postmolds were 15 to 20 cm. below floor level. The larger posts left circular molds of 35 to 40 cm. in diameter and the smaller uprights of 15 to 20 cm.

While the palisade excavations did not produce direct evidence as to what the stockade looked like above ground, some conclusions can be drawn about the direction from which the wall trenches were dug, and about the erection and destruction of the stockade walls. Large quantities of crushed swan bones were found scattered in the fill of features 26 and 27 up to three meters south of their source. Many of the bones were lying near or on the bottoms of the trenches. The source of these bones was eventually determined to be the floor of one of the Mississippian houses just below the plow zone. To explain the above circumstances, it is suggested that the bones were conveyed southward in the loose excavated earth as the trenches were moved northward. To achieve the considerable mixing of the bones the excavated earth would have to be backfilled almost immediately around logs set in the newly opened preceding section of the trench. Three specialized crews would probably be needed to dig trenches, set and align logs, and backfill. Perhaps other crews were busy adding platforms to the bastions, plastering the walls with mud, etc.

One of the bastion trenches on the other hand appears to have been excavated as a complete unit. Part of a closed, gorged bastion was cut through the other Mississippian house floor which was heavily burned. Chunks of the burned clay floor mixed in the trench fill were not displaced to any great extent and most were within the limits of the floor. The conclusion is that the excavated earth was piled on the edge until the trench was completely opened.

In all probability the stockades were dismantled and the logs reused in new walls or elsewhere. The lack of *in situ* carbonized walls and lack of evidence for large scale burning suggests the walls were not put to the torch. Direct evidence for salvaging the heavier support posts is in the form of several extraction pits on the edge of the closed gorge bastions. The general absence of postmolds, in feature 26, may mean the posts were pulled and not allowed to rot in place (for example see Wittry and Vogel, 1962: 29-30). To permit the almost complete insertion of the feature 28 trench into feature 27 between N280 and 317 the second wall would first have to be removed.

The stockade line between the test on the slough edge and the excavation south of Monks Mound when scaled from the Reeves' photographs is about 1300 lineal meters. Assuming three to four posts per meter as indicated by postmolds in feature 28 about 4,500 logs would be required to build this section alone.

Originally it was estimated the central stockade enclosed between 150 and 175 acres. The south and east sides were clearest on the aerial photographs and have since been documented by excavation. The west side is less distinct but is probably in the field east of mound 42. A strong east/west line behind Monks Mound was thought to be the northern boundary but no wall trenches were found in testing. This line probably represents a field road shown in the 1922 photographs. Continuation of the curtain trenches in unit C indicates the stockades probably cross the slough and enclose Mound 5 roughly doubling the estimated acreage for the central stockade.

The long winding trench from Tract 15A was interpreted to be the remains of a palisade which once shielded Mound 44 from the nearby village (Wittry and Vogel, 1962). The patterns of white lines around the central group of mounds at first suggested this interpretation but the discovery of bastions together with evidence from a surface collection indicates the stockades were in part defensive. In 1967 the field between Monks Mound and the projected stockade line was collected in 2.5 meter squares. While some of the sample remains to be sorted, most of the projectile points were identified and locations plotted during the survey. Most of the points were found close to the stockade line. Fowler (personal communication) has pointed out that this seeming association with the stockade line (much of which lies along the edge of the field) may be accidental and may simply reflect relic collectors pre-

ference for the center of fields. Several projectile points were recovered from
unit B, which crossed the center of the field.

There is every reason to believe that the stockades described above may
be the inner line of a defense. Continued photographic research has led to the
identification of other lines representing several possible large structural
patterns including an ultimate stockade enclosing perhaps eighty per cent of
the Cahokia site.

References Cited

Barrett, Samual A.
  1933 *Ancient Aztalan.* Bulletin of the Public Museum of the City of
        Milwaukee. Vol. 13. Milwaukee.
Black, Glenn A.
  1967 *Angel Site an Archaeological, Historical and Ethnological Study.* 2
        vol., Indiana Historical Society, Indianapolis.
Hall, Robert L.
  1968 The Goddard-Ramey Cahokia Flight: A pioneering aerial photo-
        graphic survey. *The Wisconsin Archeologist.* Vol. 49 (No. 2), pp.
        75-78. Milwaukee.
Wittry, Warren L. and Joseph O. Vogel
  1962 Illinois State Museum Projects. In *First Annual Report: American
        Bottoms Archaeology, July 1, 1961—June 30, 1962.* edited by
        Melvin L. Fowler, pp. 15-30. Illinois Archaeological Survey.
        University of Illinois, Urbana.

SOME CERAMIC PERIODS AND
THEIR IMPLICATIONS AT CAHOKIA

Patricia J. O'Brien
Kansas State University
Manhattan, Kansas

I
Ceramic Periods at Cahokia

For a number of years the ceramics at Cahokia have been grouped into two foci: Old Village and Trappist. These categories also reflect time, Old Village is early and Trappist is late. Most recently, Hall (1966:8) has suggested dates of A.D. 1050-1300 for Old Village and A.D. 1300-1550 for Trappist.

Griffin did the most important work on delineating the pottery types of these foci. Old Village is characterized by the types Powell Plain, Ramey Incised and Monks Mound Red (Griffin, 1949: 46). Trappist pottery types are St. Clair Plain, Well's Incised, Tippets Bean Pot, Cahokia Cordmarked, Cahokia Red Filmed and Salt Pans (Griffin, 1949: 46). The type-frequency method of ceramic analysis was employed in establishing these units.

As gross time markers such ceramic types are useful, but if one wishes to uncover finer time increments this approach is usually ineffective. The reason for this is that this method of analysis is statistical and while in theory these large time units can be divided into smaller ones based on the different percentages of occurrence of the types, in practice this often is impossible (Rowe, 1959: 319-30). If one excavates a grave in which three rim sherds and ten body sherds of two pottery types are found, the inadequacy of the sample makes it impossible to reliably place that grave and its materials into anything but the grossest time unit.

In an attempt to establish a more rigorous chronological sequence at Cahokia, a study was made of the ceramics from the Powell Tract section of the site excavated by Charles Bareis and Donald Lathrap (1962) using a method of analysis first developed in Classical archaeology. This approach was

100

first employed by Richter (1946) on Attic red-figured vases. By delineating the combinations of different technical and artistic attributes of these ceramics, she was able to outline five styles which existed for *ca*. 30 years each. Attic red-figured vases are a type of the same order as say Ramey Incised. The Attic vases had a duration of *ca*. 150 years; if Hall's dating is correct, Ramey Incised may span 250 years. The question then is can that 250 years be broken into smaller units using this method at Cahokia.

As implied, this method is not statistical, rather an attribute or feature is present or absent. Some features are present in one or more periods, but absent in others. With this technique one can date small ceramic samples from grave lots, pits, house floors, etc.

This method, if used, does require the acceptance of two basic assumptions which are made about the materials to be analyzed. First, we assume the pits, house floors, burials, etc. were filled rapidly probably being used as dumps in some cases (O'Brien, 1969: 18). Then as a corollary, it follows that a short period of time is represented by the pit or floor so that a particular ceramic component or phase is represented by the ceramic sample present.

The second assumption is that the potters had a finite number of ideas about pottery making and that these ideas are combined in certain consistent and non-random ways at any point in time. The assumption of a limited repertoire of ideas on ceramic manufacture within a community at any point in time means the problem is only to define these ideas for any given period. This is why the presence or absence of elements is important rather than percentages of types.

This method was used on the Powell Tract materials and six periods of occupation were uncovered. Period I was Late Woodland, the vessels were grit tempered, globular in shape with cordmarking, smoothed-over cordmarking, lip notching and wrapped-stick impressing as decorative elements. Much of this pottery is what is called early "Bluff." Period VI was an Upper Mississippian complex with collared shell tempered jars and incised parallel slashes and dents for decoration.

Periods II through V were Middle Mississippian. Period II had rolled rimmed shouldered jars, bottles, salt pans, and bowls. The Ramey Incised designs vary but the most important one is an interlocking scroll motif with attached double border rib elements. There are also two limestone tempered simple bowls.

Period III has the rims starting to unroll, and we find triangular and squarish ones, the other vessel forms continue with different rims and the Ramey interlocking scroll motif has a single border ribbed element and the scroll becomes either a circle or only a half turned scroll. There are some limestone tempered bottles, and a shouldered jar and some shallow bowls.

Period IV was not strongly represented ceramically because there was a ceremonial occupation at this time, but the shouldered jar rims have begun to flare and evert. Cups are present only in this phase while the dominant Ramey motif is a scroll and bar, and there is the further breakdown of the interlocking scroll motif.

Period V has highly everted flaring rims or extruded pinched rims on the shouldered jars. There are also shell tempered jars with cordmarking and we get the highest incidence of limestone tempered vessels (in both rim and vessel form) including the classic constricted orifice Monks Mound Red jar, also present is "stumpware." The few Ramey sherds in this period probably belong in period IV (one has a "weeping eye") because their rims are more like those of that time.

Throughout much of this Middle Mississippian occupation is found pottery which is called late "Bluff." This material is grog-grit tempered, often plain, thin walled, and generally light in core color: buffs, pinks, white, light grey, etc. Vessel forms are globular jars with four distinctive rims that occur in periods II and III. Two other rims, one flaring everted and the other extruded pinched, are in period V, and they are like two rims in the shell tempered ware. In periods II and III these vessels are only slightly shouldered in form while later ones have the rounded shoulders of the shell tempered jars.

As can be imagined, there is no direct one-to-one correlation between Powell Tract's ceramic periods and those of Griffin's foci. Powell Plain grades imperceptively into St. Clair Plain and Cahokia Red Filmed. The salt pans are early not late, the limestone tempered pottery (Monks Mound Red) runs through the sequence, and while bean pots are present in some of the early periods, the typical concave walled ones associated with Well's Incised are absent.

We should not be too surprised at this lack of correlation because given the total complexity of Cahokia and given our own small detailed knowledge on one area, we have to expect revisions as more and more of the site becomes known, and as finer and finer chronological units are isolated. One thing established in that study was that such a method of analysis is successful on this type of pottery.

But the most important thing established was a basic ceramic sequence of greater refinement into which data from various parts of the site can be integrated. These materials when set in time relationships with each other allow us to see the basic interaction and development of this culture. The sections of this paper to follow show the interaction of Cahokia with the Caddoan region and the lower Mississippi Valley region, and place some of the mound constructions in time and let us see the internal growth of the site as it relates to that phenomenon.

II
Cahokia's Relationship to the Cultures of the Caddoan Region and the Lower Mississippi Valley

For many years American archaeologists have been intrigued and plagued by the nature of the relationships between the three most important late cultural manifestations in the Eastern United States: Middle Mississippian as represented at Cahokia (Old Village and Trappist), Caddoan in the Oklahoma-East Texas-Louisiana-Arkansas region (Gibson and Fulton), and the Lower Mississippi Valley cultures (Coles Creek and Plaquemine).

A variety of interpretations of these relationships have been given in the past, but one can point out the greatest differences of opinion by presenting the two most extreme views. First, there is the view that the Lower Mississippi Valley cultures developed earliest followed in time by the appearance of Middle Mississippian culture to the north at sites like Cahokia which in turn is followed by the Caddoan manifestation. In this view, the Caddoan development is seen as being contemporary with Plaquemine. The alternate view has the Caddoan materials as the earliest and being of Mesoamerican derivation with Middle Mississippian and the Lower Mississippi Valley cultures being later in time (Newell and Krieger, 1949: 237).

It is not the intent of this paper to re-examine the old arguments *per se* or the various shades of opinion between these two extremes. The evidence is equivocal and frankly one of the major deficiencies toward establishing these associations is the lack of good comparative data set in a tight chronological framework between the ceramic sequences of these cultural groups. In some cases, there is simply no ceramic sequence with which to make such comparisons. Rather, this paper will present the evidence of contact (evidence at the very least of trade) between these regions as reflected in the recently established ceramic sequence at the Powell Tract section of the Cahokia site described above.

The following presentation will be a discussion of the trade sherds from the Caddoan and the Lower Mississippi Valley regions that were found in features and houses on the Powell Tract and were assignable to these four time units. In period II are Caddoan rim and body sherds of pottery types belonging to the Alto Focus of the Gibson Aspect. They are types Holly Fine Engraved, Hickory Fine Engraved, Davis Incised, and Bowles Creek Plain (Figs. 48-51, 55).

In the early part of period III these types of Caddoan sherds continue as Holly Fine Engraved and Bowles Creek Plain persist while Crockett Curvilinear Incised body sherds appear (Figs. 52a-i, 54a-b).   Also present in this period is a sharply angular jar rim whose paste is similar to that of the Coles Creek Incised sherds of period V, but whose only decoration is a brown

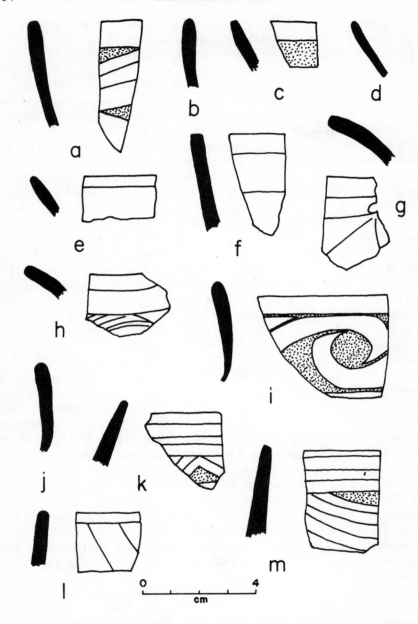

Fig. 48. Potsherds from the University of Illinois excavations in the Powell Mound area of the Cahokia site. Holly Fine Engraved (a, c, g-i, k-m), Hickory Fine Engraved (e-f), and Bowles Creek Plain (b, d, j) rim and body sherds.

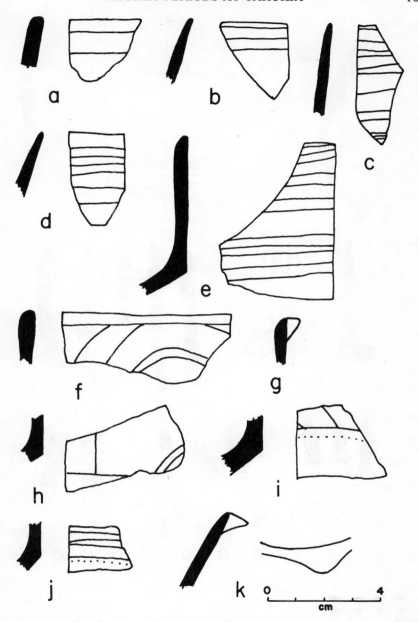

Fig. 49. Potsherds from the University of Illinois excavations in the Powell Mound area of the Cahokia site. Holly Fine Engraved (f, h-i), Hickory Fine Engraved (a-e, j), and Bowles Creek Plain (g, k) rim and body sherds.

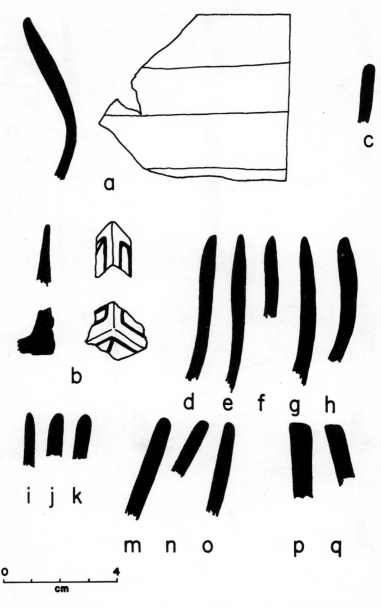

Fig. 50. Potsherds from the University of Illinois excavations in the Powell Mound Area of the Cahokia site. Holly Fine Engraved (b), Davis Incised (a), and Bowles Creek Plain (c, d-q) rim and body sherds.

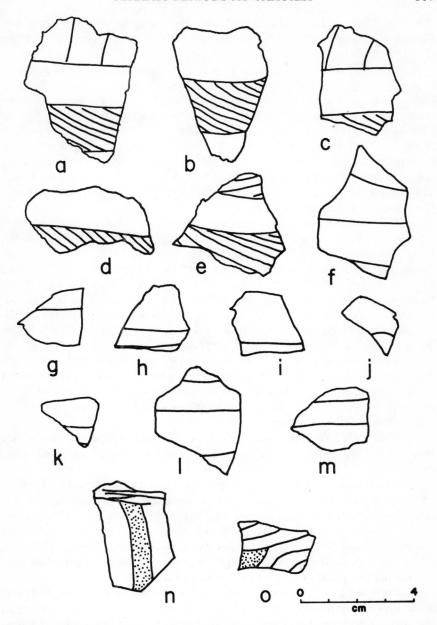

Fig. 51. Potsherds from the University of Illinois excavations in the Powell Mound area of the Cahokia site. Holly Fine Engraved (a-f, n-o), Davis Incised (g-l), and Hickory Fine Engraved (m) body sherds.

slip (Fig. 52j). It is thought that this vessel belongs to the type Larto Red
Filmed associated with Baytown, and also a diagnostic type for Troyville
(Ford, 1951:59).

At the close of period III a very unique and interesting vessel is found.
It is a very large bowl that has a grooved line on its lip and has an elaborately
engraved design on its interior (Fig. 53a, c). Dr. Clarence H. Webb (personal
communication) made the following observations about this vessel after he
examined it. "The shape and rim treatment is perfectly good Coles Creek, as
is the paste." He suggests the rim is squared and says that "the squared rim
with peaks is seen in early Caddoan ceramics . . ., but the outward folded rim
with a groove down the lip is a regular feature in French Fork Incised type."
The red slip is not as frequent in French Fork type but is reported and so is
not inconsistent with it.

The decoration though, is different as interior decorating has not been
reported on French Fork, also this vessel's design was engraved which is not
French Fork nor even a Coles Creek technique. Webb comments: "So far as
the decoration is concerned, the choice is of feather symbols of a finger and
eye decoration." Since the elements of cross band with longitudinally
bisecting line on this vessel are similar to those on a vessel from the Mounds
Plantation Site in Caddo Parish, Louisiana, Webb believes the design on the
vessel from Cahokia is also the finger rather than the feather symbol (see
Webb and McKinney, 1963: 1-9, for illustrations).

Webb concludes that ". . . we have a vessel made like French Fork, with
decoration seen heretofore only on an early Caddoan vessel and made with a
Caddoan technique . . . . This is a ceremonial vessel with finger (and eye?)
symbols, made at the time of Coles Creek-Gibson Caddoan contact or
transition and showing features of each."

The trade ceramics from period IV are very meager. There is one
Bowles Creek Plain rim, plus the addition of Dunkin Incised body sherds (Fig.
54c-e).

Finally, period V has rims of the type Coles Creek Incised (Fig. 54i-j).
These rims lack the characteristic "overhanging" of the incised line of this
type, but have the grooved incised lip. The plain lines of these vessels are
similar to those of the type Hardy Incised of the Plaquemine period, but the
grooved lip line only occurs on Coles Creek Incised type (Ford, 1951: 74,
87-88). It is thought that this "mixing" of elements indicates a period of time
transitional from Coles Creek to Plaquemine periods.

There are also some undecorated rims of shallow curved bowls that have
a red slipped surface (Fig. 54f-h, k). It is thought that these vessels belong to
the generalized type: Larto Red Filmed. This type runs throughout the Baytown period (Phillips, Ford, and Griffin, 1951: 102-104) and would seem to
have a considerable time depth or is later intrusive early material. Finally, in

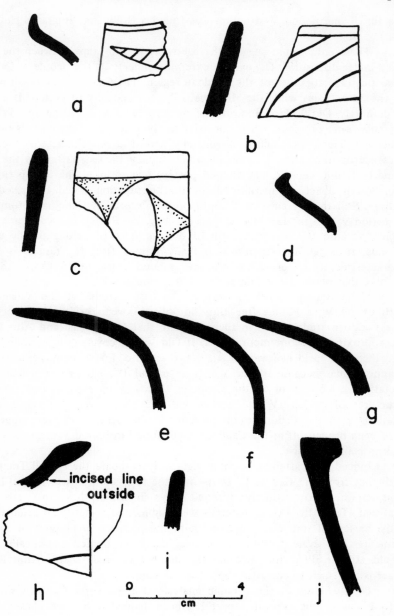

Fig. 52. Potsherds from the University of Illinois excavations in the Powell Mound area of the Cahokia site. Holly Fine Engraved (a-c), Bowles Creek Plain (d-i), and Larto Red Filmed (j) rim sherds.

the fill of one period V structure was found a Holly Fine Engraved rim (Fig. 53b).

These data would suggest the following relationships between the three areas under discussion. The earliest external connections the people at Cahokia have tie them to those of the Caddoan region. The Caddoan sherds all belong to the Alto Focus while the Middle Mississippian pottery of periods II and III is definitely Old Village. Indeed, the dichotomy of Old Village and Trappist presents some problems when one tries to fit it into the four periods isolated at Powell Tract. Old Village is generally agreed to be characterized by the presence of three pottery types of which Ramey Incised pottery is the most important. But since Ramey Incised pottery occurs in all the four periods of the Powell Tract occupation, all of that occupation could be called Old Village. Still the presence of Trappist pottery, especially Cahokia Cordmarked in period V, and the fact that there were only five Ramey Incised sherds in it, which because of their rim form or designs seem to belong to the earlier periods, it is felt that period V is really Ramey free. If Trappist is to be characterized as a period of extensive mound construction too, then it is possible that period IV is Trappist as well as number V.

Using Ramey Incised pottery as the basic criteria of Old Village but with period V as Ramey free, the Old Village covers periods II through IV. The Caddoan trade sherds in them indicate that Old Village and Alto Focus are approximately contemporaneous. If Old Village covers only periods II and III, then the evidence would suggest that Alto Focus could extend into Trappist times because of the sherds of period IV. No matter which interpretation is correct or if the Caddoan sherds were even kicked into the structures of period IV and also period V, Cahokia very early had strong relations with the Caddo region. In later times these connections appear to have been broken off as the Caddoan sherd found in period V is an early type and probably intrusive.

Indeed, any attempt to more rigorously compare the Powell Tract data with that from the George C. Davis site (the type site for Alto Focus) has to consider the two distinctly different ways in which these materials were analyzed. The Alto Focus materials were subject to a statistical arrangement while at Powell one was concerned with the presence or absence of specific elements. But even if both collections had been treated statistically there would still be difficulties because the number of trade sherds from Powell Tract is too small to constitute an adequate sample.

On the basis of the ceramic analysis at the George C. Davis site, the Alto Focus of the Gibson Aspect has been divided into three phases of occupation (Newell and Krieger, 1949). If one is willing to extend the basic assumptions made about the Cahokia pottery to that of the Davis data then certain ceramic elements on the Powell Tract trade sherds suggest some possible alignments of the two sets of data.

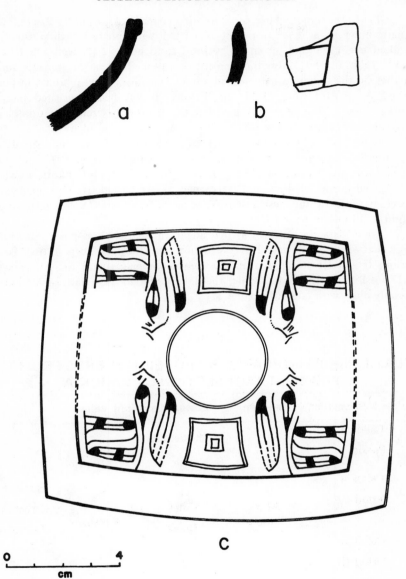

a   b

c

0 _____ 4
cm

Fig. 53. Potsherds from the University of Illinois excavations in the Powell Mound area of the Cahokia site. Engraved French Fork Exotic rim sherd and reconstruction (a,c), and a Holly Fine Engraved (b) rim sherd.

First, the interlocking scroll motif occurs in Alto phases 2 and 3; the square bowl as a vessel form is associated with phase 2 while finally, a "forked eye" is found on an effigy head from phase 2 (Newell and Krieger, 1949: Table 6, 189). Also the element of a peaked corner presumably similar to that on the unique square peaked, interior engraved bowl is found in phases 2 and 3 of Alto (*ibid*: Table 6). Finally, it has been suggested that the "forked eye" effigy head indicates that the Southern Ceremonial Complex is early in the Caddoan region (*ibid*: 160), since it occurs in phase 2.

If we look at the Powell Tract sequence we find one trade sherd with the interlocking scroll motif and it occurs in period II (Fig. 49). The square vessel form also occurs in period II while the French Fork Exotic bowl has the peaked corner element and is assigned to late period III. This same exotic vessel, because of the design motifs, suggests Southern Ceremonial Complex affinities all in late period III.

These data do not give a final alignment of the three-phase Alto Focus sequence with the Powell Tract sequence, but they do suggest that Powell periods II and III are approximately contemporaneous with the Alto phase 2 and possibly early phase, while the late Caddoan materials of period IV possibly align with late Alto phase 3.

TABLE 6

RELATIONSHIPS INDICATED BY FOREIGN SHERDS FROM THE POWELL TRACT SECTION OF CAHOKIA

Middle Mississippian	Caddoan	Lower Mississippi Valley		"Cult"
Cahokia Period V		Plaquemine		
Cahokia Period IV	. . . . . . Alto Phase 3	Coles Creek	Baytown	Southern Ceremonial Complex
Cahokia Period III	. . . . . .			
Cahokia Period II	Alto Phase 2	Troyville		
	Alto Phase 1			

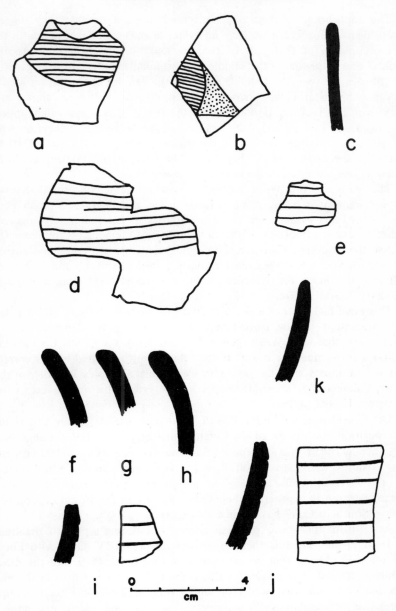

Fig. 54. Potsherds from the University of Illinois excavations in the Powell Mound area of the Cahokia site. Crockett Curvilinear Incised (a-b), Larto Red Filmed (f-h, k), Bowles Creek Plain (c), Dunkin Incised (d-e), and Coles Creek Incised (i-j) rim and body sherds.

The implications of these alignments are important because they suggest that Alto phase 1 for which we have no evidence at Powell Tract pre-dates the earliest occupation of that part of the site and by inference points to the possibility that it pre-dates the Middle Mississippian manifestation in general.

The ties between the Cahokia area and the peoples of the Lower Mississippi Valley began at Powell in period III. Interaction between Cahokia and the Baytown and Troyville populations of the Lower Mississippi Valley appear here as the Larto Red Filmed sherd indicates. Later there is a connection with the Coles Creek people further to the south at the close of period III as indicated by the exotic vessel (Fig. 52). The order of relationship would be expected as one moves from the north to the south.

The material from period III that is most intriguing concerns that vessel which for want of a better name is being called an "Engraved French Fork Exotic." This bowl would seem to have affinities to the elaborately engraved ceremonial vessels associated with the Southern Ceremonial Complex. The view that the Southern Ceremonial Complex elements are contemporaneous with the Alto Focus has been most recently restated by Webb and McKinney (1963) and it is based on an exotic, interior engraved bowl from a burial at the Mounds Plantation site.

This bowl had the eye and finger motif of "Southern Cult" and it is the stylistic treatment of the fingers and their similarity to elements on the Cahokia exotic that leads Webb (personal communication) to feel the Cahokia vessel has a finger and eye motif. If the relationship suggested here is correct then it would appear that the Southern Ceremonial Complex is earlier in the Caddoan, Cahokia and Lower Mississippi Valley regions than in the rest of the Southeastern United States.

Other evidence within the Powell Tract sequence suggesting this is the correct position for the Southern Ceremonial Complex is the presence of a Ramey Incised rim with a "weeping or forked eye" on its shoulder. This rim is from a house dating to period V, but it is probably intrusive and on the basis of rim form, really belongs in period IV. This ceramic element is important because it is generally believed to be a late manifestation occuring after the "Southern Cult" has reached its climax.

Aside from the above problem another interesting aspect of the trade wares from Powell Tract is their meagerness in period IV. Only Alto Focus sherds are assignable to that period, one a Bowles Creek Plain and the other two Dunkin Incised. The reason for this is most likely to be found in the fact that period IV is not very well represented ceramically on the tract because the presence of "ceremonial" architecture in that time zone precludes a residential occupation. Other data I have seen suggests this period is much better represented at the Mitchell site and on Tracts 15A and 15B of the Cahokia site. It is very probably that the relationship with the Lower Missis-

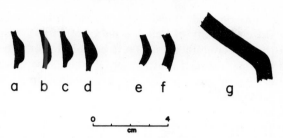

a   b c d   e f   g

0_____4
cm

Fig. 55. Potsherds from the University of Illinois excavations in the Powell Mound area of the Cahokia site. Bowles Creek Plain shoulder sherds (a-g).

sippi Valley is continued because of the presence of Baytown and Coles Creek pottery in period V even though these materials are absent in period IV.

Of the trade sherds in period V only the Coles Creek Incised rims give any data that might be chronologically useful. As stated earlier, the lack of "overhanging" on the lines, but the presence of the grooved lip line, points to a transition between the Coles Creek and Plaquemine periods. And because of this, it is felt that period V is contemporaneous with very late Coles Creek just prior to the transition into Plaquemine. The lone Caddoan rim of Holly Fine Engraved is thought to be a late intrusive that was probably kicked into the house and does not represent a true exchange between the two areas.

In summary, it would appear that the trade materials from the Powell Tract section of Cahokia indicate that Old Village, Alto (phases 2 and 3), and Coles Creek are co-terminous at the very least. There is also the suggestion that Alto (Phase 1) pre-dates Old Village and Coles Creek manifestations because it is not present on the Powell Tract, although it should be remembered that future research may locate it on other earlier parts of the Cahokia site. The evidence from period V points to the possibility that Trappist may date to terminal Coles Creek just transitional to Plaquemine. And finally, there is some evidence within the Cahokia ceramic sequence to support Webb's position that the Southern Ceremonial Complex is earlier in the Caddoan region as well as at Cahokia and in the Coles Creek area than in the rest of the Southeastern United States. Table 6 is a graphic representation of these relationships.

III
Dating Mound Construction at Cahokia

John Rowe (1959) has rightly observed that if an archaeologist wishes to study cultural process he must be able to order the evidence for that process in a chronological framework. If any true understanding of the dynamics of the community of Cahokia and of Middle Mississippian culture in general is to be achieved then one must be able to arrange the evidence of such growth in time. Mound construction, if it could be placed within a time sequence, would be of great utility for understanding the settlement pattern developments at Cahokia.

One important body of data consists of the ceramics from the mounds of Cahokia that were excavated in the 1920's by Moorehead and his associates. An analysis of this material should then allow for the establishment of the construction periods for the various mounds and to relate them to each other in time. In a previous study (O'Brien, 1969) the author analysed the pottery from the Powell Tract section of the Cahokia site, but used the Ramey Incised pottery from the Moorehead collections to supplement and fill out the analysis of Ramey Incised ceramics from Powell Tract. Specific characteristics of Ramey Incised were utilized in dividing the periods described in Section I. An examination of the Moorehead material should give information on the sequence of mound development at the site.

It is not the intent of the writer to present here the complete analysis of the Ramey pottery, but rather to tabulate the distribution of sherds with proveniences in the mounds that were a part of that original analysis. Table 7 illustrates the mound proveniences and associated catalog numbers for the sherds and shows their incidence by period.

Six mounds are represented in this collection of Ramey Incised pottery. They are the Powell Mound No. 2, the James Ramey Mound, the Edwards Mound, the Sawmill Mound, the Temple Mound near the James Ramey Mound, and finally, Mound 5, Roxana, Choteau Township. As Table 7 indicates, the Powell Mound No. 2 has Ramey pottery occurring in all four periods of the Middle Mississippian complex isolated on Powell Tract while the James Ramey Mound, the Edwards Mound, and the Sawmill Mound have ceramics from periods II through IV. Mound 5, Roxana, Choteau Township, has Ramey Incised sherds from period III.

If Period V is a post-Ramey phase then it would appear that the Powell Mound No. 2, the James Ramey Mound, the Edwards Mound, and the Sawmill Mound were constructed sometime in period IV of the Powell Tract sequence. Because the mounds were constructed with fill from the surface of the site early materials are mixed with later ones, and for this reason the mound construction dates are based on the period assignment of the latest pottery. Table 7 shows that the Temple Mound probably was built in period IV while Mound 5, Roxana, Choteau Township, was constructed in number III.

These data and conclusions must be considered as tentative because although it is reasonable to assume a random intrusion of Ramey Incised ceramics into the mound fill, the final dating of the construction of these

TABLE 7
PERIOD ASSIGNMENTS OF
MOUND PROVENIENCES FROM CAHOKIA

		II	III	IV	V
Powell Mound No. 2					
(no data)	A-4017	X	X	X	
(no data)	A-4257	X	X	X	
(no data)	A-4259	X		X	X
(no data)	A-4264	X		X	
(no data)	A-4265	X	X		
(no data)	A-4274	X	X	X	
(surface)	A-3999	X	X		
(OM)	A-4268			X	
(OM)	A-4269		X		
(L. Carey Place)	A-4263			X	
James Ramey Mound in 1922					
	A-1			X	
	A-79			X	
	A-138		X		
	A-168		X	X	
	A-386			X	
(near surface)	A-616	X	X	X	
(near surface)	A-613	X	X		
(1'-8' below summit)	A-620		X	X	
(1'-8' below summit)	A-614			X	
Edwards Mound in 1921					
	A-758	X	X	X	
Sawmill Mound in 1922					
	A-387	X	X	X	
Temple Mound, near James Ramey Mound, Spiral pit, 1922	A-634			X	
Mound 5, Roxana, Choteau Township, Cahokia Explorations 1922	A-1186		X		

structures depends on the complete analysis of all the ceramics from these mounds. This material is presented now because it would be useful to have even tentative notions about the sequence of mound construction at the site. This is especially the case for the studies of mound building based on axis orientation and lineal relationships being worked on by some archaeologists. In the light of those studies it is important to point out some of the meager evidence for dating aspects of construction operations on Monks Mound itself. A whole Ramey Incised jar was excavated from the top of Monks Mound and this vessel is believed to be associated with the last occupation of the mound top (Hall, 1966: 604). James Warren Porter (personal communication) was kind enough to have shown me this jar and on the basis of design and rim form it would date to period IV of the Ramey sequence developed for Powell Tract. This means that the final construction operations on this mound apparently occurred in period IV.

The material presented here would seem to suggest that mounds were constructed on the site of Cahokia in periods III and IV, but unit IV appears to have been a period of intensive mound erection. Whether mound construction occurred in period II remains to be established, and at what earlier date Monks Mound was first built cannot at present be ascertained.

Acknowledgements

This paper is a by-product of my doctoral dissertation entitled "A Formal Analysis of Cahokia Ceramics: Powell Tract" and submitted to the Department of Anthropology, University of Illinois. I am especially grateful to my chairman, Dr. Donald W. Lathrap for his encouragement and his critical and stimulating comments on that study and also on this paper.

I am also pleased to acknowledge a special debt to Dr. Clarence H. Webb of Shrevesport, Louisiana who identified the exotic French Fork vessel and outlined its significance (personal communication, letter dated Nov. 25, 1967). Dr. Webb also gave me some stimulating comments on the original version of this paper first read at the Society for American Archaeology meetings in Sante Fe last spring (personal communication, letter dated May 18, 1968).

I would like to thank Drs. Donald W. Lathrap and John C. McGregor of the Department of Anthropology of the University of Illinois for allowing me to use the materials from the Moorehead Collections. I would also like to thank James Warren Porter of the University of Winnipeg, Manitoba, Canada, for showing me the Ramey jar from the top of Monks Mound and allowing me to use this data.

A note is pertinent to the illustrations, all the vessel interiors are to the left of the drawings and the reconstruction of the exotic vessel is one-third the scale of the other sherds. A complete description of all the sherds used in this study will be found in the appendices of my dissertation.

Finally, I alone am responsible for any mis-interpretations of the data.

References Cited

Bareis, Charles and Donald Lathrap
    1962 University of Illinois. In: *First Annual Report: American Bottoms Archaeology*. Melvin L. Fowler (editor). *Illinois Archaeological Survey*, pp. 3-14. Urbana.

Ford, James A.
    1951 Greenhouse: A Troyville-Coles Creek Site in Avoyells Parish, Louisiana. *Anthropological Papers of the American Museum of Natural History*, Vol. 44 (pt. 1).

Griffin, James B.
    1949 The Cahokia Ceramic Complexes. *Proceedings of the Fifth Plains Conference for Archaeology*, Vol. 1, pp. 44-57. Laboratory of Anthropology, University of Nebraska, Lincoln.

Hall, Robert L.
    1966 Cahokia Chronology. Paper read at the Annual Meeting of the Central States Anthropological Society in St. Louis. pp. 1-9, 1966 (Mimeographed).
    1966 Current Research: Northern Mississippi Valley. *American Antiquity*, Vol. 31, pp. 604-609. Salt Lake City.

Menzel, Dorothy, John H. Rowe, and Lawrence E. Dawson
    1964 The Paracas Pottery of Ica. *University of California Publications in American Archaeology and Ethnology, Vol. 50*. University of California Press, Berkeley and Los Angeles.

Newell, H. Perry, and Alex D. Krieger
    1949 The George C. Davis Site, Cherokee County, Texas. *Memoirs of the Society for American Archaeology, No. 5*, Menasha.

O'Brien, Patricia J.
    1969 A Formal Analysis of Cahokia Ceramics: Powell Tract. Unpublished doctoral dissertation. University of Illinois, Urbana.

Phillips, Philip, James A. Ford, and James B. Griffin
    1951 Archaeological Survey in the Lower Mississippi Alluvial Valley, 1940-1947. *Papers of the Peabody Museum of American Archaeology and Ethnology, Harvard University, Vol. XXV*. Cambridge, Mass.

Richter, Gisela M.A.
   1946 *Attic Red-Figured Vases, A Survey.* Yale University Press. New
        Haven.
Rowe, John H.
   1959 Archaeological Dating and Cultural Process. *Southwestern Journal
        of Anthropology,* Vol. 15 (No. 4), pp. 317-24. Albuquerque.
Webb, Clarence H., and Ralph R. McKinney
   1963 An Unusual Pottery Vessel from Mounds Plantation Site, Caddo
        Parish, Louisiana. *The Arkansas Archaeologist,* Vol. IV (No. 5),
        pp. 1-9.

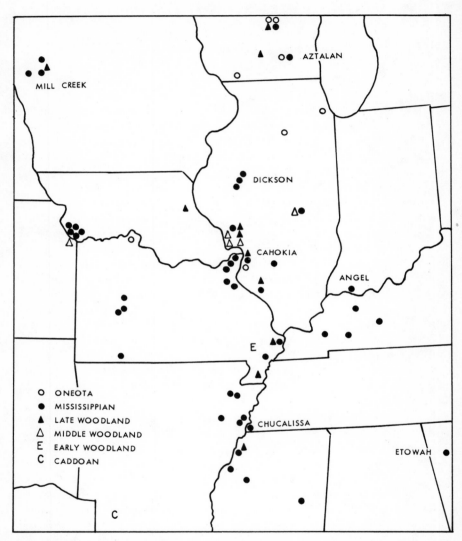

Fig. 56. The locations of sites having corn remains analysed in this report are shown in this map.

CORN FROM CAHOKIA SITES

Hugh C. Cutler and Leonard W. Blake
Missouri Botanical Garden
St. Louis, Mo.

The amount of plant material unearthed from the Cahokia area in the past few years and saved and studied is greater than that known from all previous excavations in the region. Most important are the collections of corn. The total amount of plant materials from Cahokia is still minute when one considers the size, importance, and length of occupation of the site, but we can now distinguish some major kinds of corn and detect signs of the directions of trade (Fowler, 1964, 1965).

Almost any native New World corn user in the past and recent years grew several kinds, each one kept for certain purposes and grown from seed ears selected because they conformed to definite standards. Ideally we should find and compare caches of selected lots of corn representing each of the kinds distinguished by the inhabitants. This would show what they considered the ideal within the range of the kinds grown at Cahokia. In addition we would like to find large masses from granaries, to show us what was the range of variation in the fields of single kinds of corn, and to suggest the effect of environment and agricultural techniques on their crops. To do this effectively we would need some collections of stalks and root systems so we could tell whether nubbin ears in a harvest were the result of unusual bad growing years or poorly tended fields, or whether they came from supplementary ears above and below the usual ears of a plant, or were borne on tillers or suckers.

Caches and large lots of ears from storage pits, or storage areas in houses are rare, although they are undoubtedly more common than our data suggest. Even when a storage structure or a house containing a seed cache was burned, the corn probably did not become thoroughly carbonized. For example, at a site at the mouth of Antire Creek, west of St. Louis, we examined several black rings visible in the cut face. These were formed by the upper third of carbonized corn kernels. The number of rows of grains present on the original ear and the size of the ear could easily be seen in the profile. By cutting at right angles to the exposed cross section, a measurement of kernel thickness could be obtained. If this material was excavated without recognizing and studying it or making a record of it in the face, it would be difficult to even recognize the thin carbonized grain surfaces as corn, and there would be no

123

TABLE 8
CORN FOUND WITHIN THE CAHOKIA SITE

(All cobs carbonized — not adjusted for shrinkage)

Site and Excavator	Date and Culture	Mean Row No.	Median Cupule Width in mm.	No. Cobs	Row Numbers % Total Cobs				
					8	10	12	14	16+
Top of Monks Md. (11Ms38) C. J. Bareis	c. 1110±150 Miss.	10.4	5.2	10	20	40	40	–	–
Monks Md. (11Ms38) S. Terrace C. J. Bareis	c. 1300 ? Miss. ?	8.9	7.9	40	65	28	7	–	–
Md. 19 G. Perino	c. 1150, Miss.	11.1	7.5	9	22	22	34	22	–
Under Md. 31 J. R. Caldwell	c. 1100-1200 Miss.	12.0	6.4	1	–	–	100	–	–
Under Md. 34 G. Perino	c. 1150±110 Miss.	11.9	6.4	27	7	19	48	22	4
Pit under Md. 51, (11S34-2) W. Chmurny, C. J. Bareis	c.1000 Miss.	12.5	7.0	15	–	13	60	13	13
Ramey Md. from depth of 8ft. E. Herold	c. 1200 ? Miss.	16.0	6.0	1	–	–	–	–	100
Under Kunneman Md. (11MsII) P. Holder	c. 800-1100 Miss.	12.3 Also 8, 10, 12-rowed corn grains	6.5	46	–	20	56	15	9

Site / Investigator	Date	Culture									Notes
15A, 3000 ft. W. Monks Md. W. Wittry & R. Hall	c. 825-1375	L. Woodland & Miss	10.8	6.8	69	17	29	50	4	–	
15B, 800 ft. W. of Monks Md. W. Wittry and R. Hall	c. 875-1545	L. Woodland & Miss.	10.7	6.9	64	13	48	31	6	2	
Powell tract (11Ms2-2) D. Lathrap	c. 620-1055	L. Woodland & Miss.	10.8	6.6	15	6	47	47	–	–	Slightly crescent corn grains
Ramey Farm, just E. of Monks Md. G., Perino & J. Tarr	c. 900-1100	Miss.	12.3	6.0	7	29	–	43	14	14	
Grove Borrow Pit (11Ms2-2) C. J. Bareis	c. 620-1055	L. Woodland & Miss.	11.8	7.4	18	–	44	45	11	–	Corn grains, not crescent shape
Bower, 3/4 mi. W. Monks Md. J. Bower	c. 1200 ?	Miss.	12.0	6.3	2	–	–	100	–	–	
Master Feed (11S34-5) C. J. Bareis	c. 850±210	Miss.									8, 10, 12-rowed corn grains Medium to small
Collinsville Airport (11S34) C. J. Bareis	c. 1085-1435	Miss.	11.3	7.0	19	11	26	53	11		
Fingerhut, 1-1/2 mi. S. W. Monks Md., C. J. Bareis	c. 1000+ ?	Miss.									8-rowed corn grain

way to tell what kind of corn it was. The major portion of the grains and all of the cob, all uncarbonized, had rotted away and been replaced with soil. Flotation and similar methods recover many specimens usually missed, but are no subsitute for careful and intelligent excavation.

Most material from Cahokia sites has been carefully labeled so that found with burials, in containers, in special areas of significant structures, etc., can be given special attention.

It is usually impossible to give good dates at the time a site is dug and the specimens are placed in the field sacks, but wherever possible, a label should state that a lot comes from above, on, or under a floor, or from a certain level so that comparisons may be made with specimens above or below, possibly later or earlier in time, but likely to be of different time periods and distinct harvests and perhaps of different kinds. Even rough indications of period are useful. Accurate dates make possible useful comparisons with related sites, but good stratigraphy enables us to see what changes occur during the lifetime of a site.

General collections of corn are seldom representative of the kinds grown at a site. Larger cobs are the first to be picked up to use as tools or fuel. Small cobs, broken fragments of soft and large cobs, and small ears borne in the tassels sift to the bottom of the pile and are often the last to be burned. In a fire, the upper and larger ears in a pile may burn completely because they are exposed to the air while the smaller specimens at the bottom are heated away from the air and gradually turn into carbon. The opposite is true of smoke pits, such as many which Carl Chapman extracted entire from the historic, Little Osage, Johnson Site (23VE4) of 1775-1820, and shipped to us in burlap and plaster jackets so that we could study the disposition of the cobs. In these smoke pits, practically all the cobs are large and broken while the general rubbish from several refuse pits contained a wide range of cob sizes including many which were far smaller than those found in the smoke pits.

Small cobs and the softer kinds of large ones are often destroyed or broken into small fragments by trampling so it is essential to study these as well as the larger fragments and entire cobs and ears. Fortunately, even small fragments, sometimes pieces less than a quarter of an inch across, can tell something about the kind of ear they came from. Such fragments are now being recovered, often by flotation methods (Struever, 1968) from sites which would otherwise usually yield little or no corn.

Oldest corn from the Cahokia area is mainly small and 12-rowed. Such are the collections from the Kane site, under the Kunnemann mound, and the pit under Mound 51, Cahokia (Tables 8 and 9). This oldest corn is a very hard flint or pop similar to the Mexican races (Wellhausen and others, 1952) Chapalote, Reventador, and Nal-Tel. This kind is found in some Hopewell and

TABLE 9

CORN FROM SITES IN THE AMERICAN BOTTOM

(All cobs carbonized – not adjusted for shrinkage)

Site and Excavator	Date and Culture	Mean Row No.	Median Cupule Width in mm.	No. Cobs	Row Numbers % Total Cobs				
					8	10	12	14	16+
Stolle Quarry G. Perino	c. 1400	10.0	6.0	1	–	100	–	–	–
Loyd (Ms^V 74) R. Hall	c. 1310±110 or earlier L. Woodland & Miss.	11.1	6.7	63	10	38	43	8	1
Horseshoe Lake G. Perino	c. 900-1100 Early Miss.	12.0	5.7	1	–	–	100	–	–
McDonough Lake, Bluff Site G. Perino	c. 1085 L. Woodland & Miss.	11.2	5.9	5	–	40	60	–	–
Wilson Md. P. Holder	c. 1000+ Miss.	11.7 8, 10, 12-rowed corn grains	6.4	7	–	43	43	–	14
McCain (20-B4-26), Caseyville J. W. Porter	c. 1000+ ? Miss. ?	8-rowed corn grains							
Kane (11Ms194) R. Hall & P. Munson	c. 900-1050 Late Woodland	12.2	6.0	80	6	20	46	13	15
Mitchell (20B-2-3) J. W. Porter	c. 1000-1200 Miss.	? 8, 10, 12-rowed corn grains	6.4	1					

TABLE 10
CORN FROM SITES OUTSIDE THE AMERICAN BOTTOM AND WITHIN 400 MILES OF CAHOKIA
(All cobs carbonized — not adjusted for shrinkage)

Site, County, State and Excavator	Date and Culture	Mean Row No.	Median Cupule Width in mm.	No. Cobs	Row Numbers % Total Cobs				
					8	10	12	14	16+
Plum Island (11Ls2), La Salle Co., Illinois, E. Herold	c. 1500-1600 Kaskaskia (?)	9.7	7.4 Also 59 Corn grains	17	38	41	20	1	–
Lawhorn, Craighead Co., Ark. Mosalage, R. Marshall	c. 1550 Miss.	11.7	6.8	7	–	29	71	–	–
Hoxie Farm (11Ck), Cook Co., Ill. D. Pedrick, E. Herold	c. 1550 Oneota	9.8 10 corn grains	–	–	40	30	30	–	–
Banks, Crittenden Co., Ark. G. Perino	c. 1535±150 Miss.	11.0	5.4	51	4	47	43	6	–
Parkin, Cross Co., Ark. G. Perino	c. 1535±150 Miss.	10.0	8.3	2	–	100	–	–	–
Barton Ranch, Crittenden Co., Ark., G. Perino	c. 1535±150 Miss.	10.1	7.3	20	30	35	35	–	–
Chucalissa, Stratum I. Memphis, Shelby Co., Tenn., C. Nash	c. 1350-1600 Miss.	11.7	6.2	135	7	29	44	13	7
Chas. MacDuffie, Craighead Co., Ark., F. J. Soday	c. 1400 Miss.	12.0	6.3	26	4	23	46	23	4
Angel Mds., Warrick Co., Ind. J. H. Kellar	c. 1300-1500 Miss.	9.6	7.2	56	44	34	18	2	2
Guthrie (23Sa131), Saline Co., Mo. D. R. Henning	c. 1450±60 Oneota	9.4	7.5	7	56	14	29	–	–

Site	Date								
Lyon's Bluff (220k1), Oktibbeha Co., Miss., R. A. Marshall	c. 1200-1500 Miss.	10.8	6.1	78	10	46	39	4	1
Buford, Tallahatchee Co., Miss. R. A. Marshall	c. 1200-1500 Miss.	9.0	8.1	2	50	50	—	—	—
15Ly18a, Lyon Co., Ky. D. Schwartz	c. 1300+ Miss.	10.2	7.8	12	42	17	33	8	—
15Ch2, Christian Co., Ky. D. Schwartz	c. 1300+ Miss.	10.8	5.7	22	9	45	41	5	—
Lester Place, Lafayette Co., Ark., Lemley Coll. thru G. Perino	c. 1200-1400 Caddoan	13.7	5.6	6	—	—	33	50	17
Emmonds, Fulton Co., Ill. D. Morse	c. 1200-1400 Miss.	110 corn grains, mostly from 8-rowed ears							
Crosno, Mississippi Co., Mo. S. Williams	c. 1200-1400 Miss.	10.1	6.8	18	28	39	33	—	—
Boyce (23Jo40), Jefferson Co., Mo., R. M. Adams	c. 1200-1400 Miss.	12.0	5.2	1	—	—	100	—	—
		11.1 (grains)		34	18	32	35	9	6
Cedar Row, Dickson Mds., Fulton Co., Ill., J. Caldwell & P. Munson	c. 1300±100 Miss	9.5	7.2	14	29	50	21	—	—
Larson (11F1109) Fulton Co., Ill. P. Munson thru R. Hall	c. 1300± Miss.	10.7	5.6	3	67	33	—	—	—
Turner — Snodgrass (23Bu21) Butler Co., Mo., J. Price	c. 1300 Miss.	10.8	6.3	51	6	49	35	8	2
15ML4, McLean Co., Ky. D. Schwartz	c. 1200+ Miss.	12.5	6.5	20	5	25	30	20	20
15Bt20, Butler Co., Ky. D. Schwartz	c. 1200+ Miss.	11.8	6.5	8	—	37	38	25	—

TABLE 10 (Continued)

CORN FROM SITES OUTSIDE THE AMERICAN BOTTOM AND WITHIN 400 MILES OF CAHOKIA

(All cobs carbonized — not adjusted for shrinkage)

Site, County, State and Excavator	Date and Culture	Mean Row No.	Median Cupule Width in mm.	No. Cobs	Row Numbers % Total Cobs					
					8	10	12	14	16+	
Etowah, Md. "C", Bartow Co., Ga. L. H. Larson, Jr.	c. 1050-1400 Miss.	8.4	7.3	64	78	22	–	–	–	
Jasper Newman (11Ks4), F 21, F 37, Moultrie Co., Ill., W. M. Gardner	c. 1000-1400 Miss.	10.5	7.6	13	23	53	8	8	8	
Vandiver Md. "B", (23P16) Platte Co., Mo., J. M. Shippee	c. 1290±80 Miss.	Corn grains from 8, 10 and 12-rowed ears								
Bornick, Green Lake Co., Wisc. G. G. Gibbon	c. 1290 Oneota	Corn grains from 8, 10 and possibly 12-rowed ears								
McClarnon (23P16) Platte Co., Mo. J. M. Shippee	c. 1260±90 Miss.	9.0	8.0	4	50	50	–	–	–	
Dietz, Dane Co., Wisc. D. A. Baerreis	c. 1250 L. Woodland	12.0	6.5	1	–	–	100	–	–	
Walker-Hooper (47GL65), Green Lake Co., Wisc., G. G. Gibbon	c. 1200-1250 Oneota	9.9	6.0	19	53	21	10	16	–	
White R., Near mouth James R. (23Sn42) Stone Co., Mo., W. R. Wood Miss.	c. 1100±400	12-14 rowed cob, C. W. 7.0 mm. "May be mixture early corn and N. flint."								
47GL122, Green Lake Co., Wisc. W. Wittry	c. 1100-1200 L. Woodland & Miss.	10.7	?	3	67	33	–	–	–	
Midway (47La19), Lafayette Co., Wisc., R. Peske	c. 1100-1200 Oneota	Grains from 8 and 10-rowed ears								

Site	Date / Culture								
Lasley's Point (47Wn8, 16) Winnebago Co., Wisc., R. Peske	c. 1100-1200 Oneota	Corn grains from 8, 10, 12 and one 14-rowed ear							
Beals (13Ck62) Cherokee Co., Iowa D. R. Henning	c. 1100-1200 L. Woodland	Corn grains from 8, 10 and 12-rowed ears Most wider than long							
Friend and Foe (23CL113) Clay Co. Mo., F. A. Calabrese	c. 1100±110 Miss.	Grains and cupules from 8, 10 and a few 12-rowed ears Not extreme N. flint							
Meyer, St. Louis Co., Mo. W. O. Meyer	c. 1000-1200 ? L. Woodland & Miss.	10.0	?	3	33	33	33	—	—
Antire Creek (23SL62) St. Louis Co., Mo., L. W. Blake	c. 1000-1200 ? Miss.	10.2	6.0	22	18	59	18	5	—
Jep Long (23Jv35) Jefferson Co., Mo., R. M. Adams	c. 1000-1200 ? Miss.	12.0 (cob) 9.1 (grains)	6.0	1 61	24	15	100	—	—
Mansker (24-A2-8) Randolph Co., Ill., J. W. Porter	c. 1000-1200 ? Miss.	11.2	6.8	36	17	22	44	17	—
Steed-Kisker (23PL13) Platte Co. Mo., J. M. Shippee	c. 1080±80 Miss.	9.0	6.8	2	50	50	—	—	—
Hays (22Co612), Coahoma Co., Miss. J. M. Connaway	c. 1000-1200 Miss.	11.6	6.4	14	7	29	50	7	7
Phipps (13Ck21) Cherokee Co., Iowa	c. 810-1350 Miss.	11.8	5.5	24	33	8	38	21	—
130b4, O'Brien Co., Iowa D. R. Henning	c. 810-1350 Miss.	10.5	5.0	2	50	—	—	—	50
Kimball (13Pm4) Plymouth Co., Iowa, D. R. Henning	c. 810-1350 Miss.	10.5	5.3	16	25	31	38	6	—
River Bend East (23SL79) Ho. #1, St. Louis Co., Mo., D. R. Henning	c. 800-1200 ? L. Woodland & Miss.	• 8, 10, 12-rowed medium sized grains. Not extreme crescent shape.							

Note (Antire Creek): Based on 3 cobs; 8, 10, 14-rowed and 18 grains

TABLE 10 (Continued)

CORN FROM SITES OUTSIDE THE AMERICAN BOTTOM AND WITHIN 400 MILES OF CAHOKIA

(All cobs carbonized — not adjusted for shrinkage)

Site, County, State and Excavator	Date and Culture	Mean Row No.	Median Cupule Width in mm.	No. Cobs	Row Numbers % Total Cobs				
					8	10	12	14	16+
River Bend East (23SL79) Pit St. Louis Co., Mo., D. R. Henning	c. 800-1200 ? L. Woodland & Miss.	Six 8 and two 10-rowed grains, mainly crescent, but longer than usual for N. flint.							
Schild, Greene Co., Ill. G. Perino	c. 1050-1150 L. Woodland & Miss.	About 150 small to medium sized grains, a few 10-rowed. Most unmeasurable.							
Texas No. 1 (21B-3-6) Clinton Co., Ill., R. Morrell	c. 1030-90± Miss.	10.0	6.2	112	29	46	21	4	–
Carcajou Point (47Je2), Jefferson Co., Wisc., R. Peske	c. 1000 Oneota	10.7	7.0	30	7	53	37	3	–
Aztalan (47Jel), Jefferson Co., Wisc., J. E. Freeman	c. 1000 Miss.	12.0	6.0	1	–	–	100	–	–
Chucalisia, Stratum III, Memphis, Shelby Co., Tenn., C. Nash	c. 1000 Miss.	11.8	6.3	13	–	23	62	15	–
Button Cairn (23Hi208) Hickory Co., Mo., R. T. Bray	c. 1000 ? Miss.	Thirteen grains from 8-rowed ear, two from 10-rowed, medium 8, 0-9.5 mm. wide.							
Madrigal Md. (23Po300) Polk Co., Mo., W. R. Wood	c. 1000 ? Miss.	8.0	11.8	1	100				
		Grains from 8, 10, 12-rowed ears							
Kings Curtain Md. (23Po307) Polk Co., Mo., W. R. Wood	c. 1000 ? Miss.	Three quarts corn grains mostly from 8 and 10-rowed and a few from 12-rowed ears.							
Marty Coolidge (21C-1-18) Randolph St. Clair Co. line, Ill., C. Kuttroff	c. 1000 L. Woodland	10.5	6.0	23	26	26	44	4	–

Site	Date / Culture	Remarks								
Warren Gresham (23PL48) Platte Co., Mo. J. M. Shippee	c. 875±150 Miss.	One 12-rowed ear. Grains small, slightly large and flattened for pop.								
Bond's (22Tu530), Tunica Co., Miss., J. M. Connaway	c. 800-900 L. Bayton & Miss.		12.0	6.4	7	–	29	43	28	–
McColloch (23Nm252) New Madrid Co., Mo., R. A. Marshall	c. 800 ? Miss.	Grains from 8, 10 and 12-rowed ears 8-rowed wider than long; 12-rowed longer than wide.								
Popke (23Mn302) Marion Co., Mo. D. R. Henning	c. 800 – L. Woodland	20 grains, 2/3 medium from 10-12 rowed ears. 1/3 small 12-14 rowed thin and narrow.								
Kersey (23Pm42) Pemiscot Co., Mo., R. A. Marshall	c. 800 – Baytown	Corn grains from 12 to 14 rowed ears. Small flint or medium pop.								
Hoecake (23Mi8) Mississippi Co., Mo., R. Williams	c. 800 – ? Early to late Baytown	(Cupules only)	11.3	5.2	3	–	33	67	–	–
Apple Creek (11Ge2) Greene Co., Ill., S. Struever	c. 350-650 L. Woodland	NOT CARBONIZED – POSSIBLY MODERN	12.0	5.1	1	–	–	100	–	–
Peisker, Calhoun Co., Ill. S. Struever	c. 100-400 M. Woodland	Also pop corn grains, probably 14 rowed	12.5	5.6	8	–	75	25	–	–
Trowbridge (14Wy1), Wyandotte Co., Kansas, N. R. Manion	c. 100-400 ? M. Woodland	One 10-rowed ear, 6.5 mm. C. W. Moderately thickened cob, less than N. flints, but not an open early type cupule								
Ansell (11Ca17) Calhoun Co., Ill. J. C. McGregor	? M. Woodland ?	106 corn grains, mostly from 12-rowed ears. A few 10 or 14-rowed and one 16-rowed.								
Jasper Newman (11Ks4), F 13, F 18, Moultrie Co., Ill., W. M. Gardner	c. 90± M. Woodland		10.0	7.0	9	45	22	22	11	–
Macoupin Creek, Jersey Co., Ill., S. Struever	c. A.D. 1 ± M. Woodland	One 12-rowed ear								
Tom Baker, Stoddard Co., Mo., R. A. Marshall	c. 100 B.C. Late Early Woodland	Two corn grains, one from 8 and one from 10-rowed ear.								

Mill Creek sites and persisted until historic times when very small amounts were grown by practically all Indian groups north of Mexico. In the last 100 years, pop and extremely hard flint varieties have been less important and relatively few Indians grow popcorn and very small flint corn today.

Most recent corn from the Cahokia area is the Northern Flint race. This is an 8-rowed corn with greatly thickened and enlarged cobs, with kernels as broad as long, and with greatly enlarged shanks (Brown and Anderson, 1947). There also were flour and probably sweet forms of the same race. Eight-rowed corn goes back at least to Hopewell times (Prufer and others, 1965: 109) and is known from early sites in the Southwest and Southeast. In the Southeast, it may have been the major kind of corn as early as three or four hundred A.D. Early forms have softer and smaller cobs and a gradient can be observed in distance and time from softer and earlier 8-rowed corn of the Southwest to more recent, extremely hard, late corn of eastern and northeastern United States.

Occasional 8-rowed ears are frequently borne on the upper parts of many-eared corn plants because upper ears tend to have fewer rows of grains. Similarly, when adverse growing conditions result in smaller plants, there is an increase in the number of 8-rowed ears. Such ears are small, frequently only partially pollinated, and can usually be distinguished from the corn crop grown under the usual conditions.

Eight-rowed ears were not abundant until very late periods of Cahokia. Corn from a cache on the south terrace of Monks Mound (Table 8) is nearly identical to the Northern Flint corn grown in historic times by the Fox Indians at Tama, Iowa. The cobs are as large as those of modern corn and are the extremes for Cahokia, although occasional cobs from other locations reach this size. The cache apparently is a selected lot.

In general, Cahokia corn is more conservative and more southern in its characters than corn from other sites in the region. This may reflect the retention of old varieties which we have found typical of kivas and medicine bags in the Southwest (unpublished data) or continued connections with areas to the south (see, for example, the corn from Chucalissa, Memphis, Tennessee, in Table 10), or growing conditions and techniques slightly better than those prevailing in this region.

Cahokia corn, then, follows a general pattern for this region, with the earliest corn being many-rowed, small, hard flint or pop corn. Slightly later, there appear some 8-rowed ears which become more common as time goes on. There is a gradual increase in hardness and size of ears. The trend from many-rowed to 8-rowed ears and towards harder and larger ears is gradual, a result of environmental and human selection, within the kinds grown in the region and the kinds introduced, apparently mainly from the south and west. There is no evidence of sudden acceptance of new kinds of corn. Very few kinds of corn can be moved rapidly from low latitudes to higher ones because most kinds of corn are strictly adjusted to certain lengths of day. If a southern corn is moved to a higher latitude, it matures later, when the days are shorter. If the move is too great, the plant will not flower in time to produce mature and viable seed before killing frosts occur.

There is a strange scarcity of corn from the time of Hopewell culture to about the time of Mississippian emergence, roughly about A.D. 300 to A.D. 800. This corresponds roughly to the period of Georgetown phase in the Mogollon area (A.D. 500-A.D. 700) when the volume of corn recovered was greatly reduced and the amounts of wild plant material increased (Martin and others, 1952: 469). This may reflect a change in climate. Yarnell's (1964: 121-125) list of collections shows few collections in this period. By the time of the next period of climate slightly unfavorable for corn, perhaps about A.D. 1200, 8-rowed strains had evolved and were grown widely enough so they could replace the earlier 12-rowed kinds. These older kinds continued to be grown farther south, as at Chucalissa, and on favorable sites with good soils where advanced agricultural techniques could be applied.

References Cited

Brown, William L. and Edgar Anderson
    1947 The Northern Flint Corns. *Annals of the Missouri Botanical Garden*, Vol. 34, pp. 1-28, St. Louis, Missouri.

Fowler, Melvin L.
    1964 *Second Annual Report: American Bottoms Archaeology*, July 1, 1962–June 30, 1963. The Illinois Archaeological Survey, University of Illinois, Urbana, Illinois.

    1965 *Third Annual Report: American Bottoms Archaeology*, July 1, 1963–June 30, 1064. The Illinois Archaeological Survey, University of Illinois, Urbana, Illinois.

Martin, Paul S., John B. Rinaldo, Elaine Bluhm,
    Hugh C. Cutler and Roger Grange, Jr.
    1952 Mogollon Cultural Continuity and Change. *Fieldiana: Anthropology*. Vol. 40, pp. 1-528. Chicago.

Prufer, O.H., D.H. McKenzie, O. Pi-Sunyer,
    H.C. Cutler, R.A. Yarnell, P.W. Parmalee and D.H. Stansbery
    1965 *The McGraw Site; a study in Hopewellian Dynamics.* Scientific Publications of the Cleveland Museum of Natural History, New Series, Vol. 4 (No. 1), pp. 107-112. Cleveland.

Struever, Stuart
  1968 Flotation Techniques for the Recovery of Small-Scale Archae-
       ological Remains. *American Antiquity,* Vol. 33 (No. 3), pp.
       353-362. Salt Lake City.
Wellhausen, E.J., L.M. Roberts and E. Hernandez X
  in collaboration with P.C. Mangelsdorf
  1952 *Races of Maize in Mexico.* The Bussey Institution of Harvard
       University, Cambridge.
Yarnell, Richard Asa
  1964 *Aboriginal Relationships between Culture and Plant Life in the
       Upper Great Lakes Region,* Anthropological Papers, Museum of
       Anthropology, University of Michigan, Ann Arbor, No. 23.

THE MITCHELL SITE
AND PREHISTORIC EXCHANGE SYSTEMS
AT CAHOKIA: AD 1000±300

James Warren Porter
University of Wisconsin
Madison, Wisc.

Introduction

Much of the archaeological data from the Cahokia region remains unpublished. A quick glance at recent textbooks on North American prehistory reveals a sad state of affairs in so far as appraisals of Cahokia are concerned (Willey, 1966: 294-295, Figs. 5-47; and Jennings, 1968: 218, Fig. 6.35). In this paper I would like to present some of the data from the Mitchell site excavations (1960-62) which will be useful to those studying the broader problems of Cahokia area culture history.

Following a sample of details from the Mitchell site excavations (Figs. 1 and 57), I wish to present my interpretations of the Mitchell site and its relationship to the Cahokia region. It is unfortunate that a definitive descriptive analysis of the Mitchell site is not yet available. Rather than continue to refer to this data as "yet unpublished," I have considered it more useful to present a portion of the details.

During the period A.D. 1000±300, considering the magnitude of the Cahokia site, it would appear that some types of exchange systems were present, these being only one part of total economic complexity for the area. My particular interest in exchange systems stems from an attempt to interpret the Mitchell site data as a satellite community to "downtown" Cahokia. This excursion into economic anthropology is possibly premature, but in order to understand the Mitchell site I have had to attempt a model of the economic conditions for the period around A.D. 1000.

From the literature of economic anthropology I have freely used ideas from Polanyi, Nash, Gabel, Chapman, and Wright. Where pertinent to my discussion I shall insert their views with whatever changes I feel necessary to adjust the economic view to my way of thinking. Before doing this, it is appropriate to elaborate to some degree on the works of Polanyi and Nash.

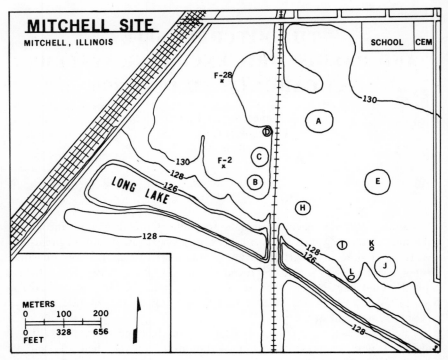

Fig. 57. Map of the Mitchell site. The only portion of the Mitchell site remaining is the area around Mound A and up to the schoolhouse. The contour is 2 meters, the elevations given are meters above sea level.

One thing obvious from the beginning was that I could not explore all of the economic potential in the archaeological data which already exists for the Cahokia region. In time it will be possible to assimilate the archaeological data from Cahokia into a view encompassing all aspects of economic life at this great center. As Nash has suggested, we could investigate four distinctive areas of primitive economics: (1) technology and labor, (2) social organization of productive units, (3) control of wealth and capital, and (4) systems and media of exchange (not his order) (Nash, 1966: 20). I have chosen to explore the systems of exchange with only passing comments on the media of exchange that might have existed in Cahokia.

The types of exchange systems have been discussed by Polanyi (1953) and I choose to use his concepts of (a) reciprocal, (b) redistribution, and (c) market economies. Nash, in addition to these three, has suggested that a fourth, mobilization exchange, should be distinguished. Dalton's (1968) review of Nash does not see mobilization exchange as a separate form of Polanyi's redistribution. It is only a special form of the redistributive system and I have treated it in the same manner.

In addition to the material consulted above, I have also found it useful to draw information from views of early markets and traders as they were seen by the Spanish. Besides Gibson (1964) and Soustelle (1964), I found a paper by Anne Chapman (1957) to be stimulating. Her paper was revealing in the areas where one wishes to see how ports of trade functioned and how the *pochteca* figured into the economic life of the larger urban centers of Tenochtitlan.

I have also attempted, where necessary, to introduce Nash's analysis of the contemporary systems in Mexico in peasant economics. His three types of economic organization all express varying degrees of interaction with a modern market system. Nash's three are (a) quasi-tribal, (b) adjunct export, and (c) regional market (Nash, 1966:60). In this contemporary situation it is clear that no one type is isolated and distinct, but rather that we are dealing with a graded system, all related to the effect of a national economy and the modern market system.

In my efforts to reconstruct possible exchange systems for the Cahokia region, I thought it useful to make use of this variety of data. Nash's various types of economies, it seems to me, should be projected back in time, if we are to believe the picture that emerges in reading Chapman, Gibson, and Soustelle. The point here is that, if we accept a complex picture existing now under the type of complex economic system which we can document clearly, and see various tribes still practicing the types of life so appealing to anthropologists, why can we not, when seeing a complex system already in existence in the 1500's, visualize similar situations for people related to centers such as Teotihuacan in Mexico or Cahokia. The *pochteca* and the markets described by the early Spanish were not only impressive, but certainly not a late development. The degree of specialization in the satellite towns to Tenochtitlan also must be viewed as having some time depth (see Gibson, 1964: 335-367).

Although I have looked primarily to the south of Cahokia from which I believe many influences were imported, Wright's papers (1967; 1968) were useful for a view toward the north of Cahokia. Wright's study provides a picture of the situation to the north of Cahokia at the time of historic contact. In his work I have found items that allow one to better reconstruct a "realistic" view of the events around Cahokia.

One colleague, in reading over my draft, pointed out that Polanyi, in using his three types of economic integration did not visualize it as an evolutionary scheme. Polanyi would conclude that our prehistoric urban centers could have developed with only the complexity of the redistributive type of system. I would suggest that this is one possible view. Another, as hinted at by Nash (1966: 33) is that we may well be dealing with a "historical sequence" from "reciprocity to redistribution to market." I tend to agree with the last scheme and have employed it here.

In short, I will attempt to develop a picture of economic exchange systems which will assist in interpreting the data accumulated by me since 1960. It will be based on a combination of the works and ideas of Polanyi, Nash, Chapman, and Wright.   Following a portion of the Mitchell site data, I shall first give an interpretation of the site as it existed through a relatively restricted time period. Then I wish to expand and employ the ideas to Cahokia in general after taking an overall look at Midwestern prehistory in terms of the scheme that I visualize. In the last section I have made a thrust into more speculations using as a base the works of colleagues working in and around Cahokia.

Potential in the Mitchell Site Data

The Mitchell site excavation is valuable to American Bottoms archaeology because the site appears to represent a satellite community to the main "downtown" Cahokia group (Fig. 56). For the midcontinent in prehistoric times it might not be too unbelievable to refer to Cahokia and its locale as an emerging prehistoric *megalopolis*.

Typical of the time, A.D. 1000, around Cahokia a great deal of energy was expended for mound construction as well as for the construction of stockades and the repeated rebuilding of small and large structures. This great amount of rebuilding activity on the part of the aboriginal inhabitants seriously disturbs the earlier evidence of other activities. This presents additional problems of interpretation to those who have worked in "downtown" Cahokia. The Mitchell site, so far as excavation is concerned, was a far simpler situation since there were seldom instances where prehistoric disturbance had seriously interrupted earlier features.

My view is that the Mitchell site was occupied for a relatively short period of time and that the main occupation of the site represents a period of only 100 years, if that much. The data to be presented documents this idea of a short time occupation. One of the primary problems with Cahokia archaeology, as I see it, revolves around the tendency to read a substantial amount of time into any clear case of stratigraphy. I am aware of the reliability of good stratigraphy at a number of sites in and around Cahokia excavated by colleagues and myself. The question of the *amount* of time between "earlier" phases and "later" phases within a site is one that I have repeatedly raised.

At Mitchell, I recognize an earlier "Bluff" occupation as well as the occasional Archaic tool, but the difference in time between the Bluff people and the main occupation of the site is not clear. It is in these types of sites where we see problems in utilizing Carbon-14 interpretations. Some colleagues emphasize various pottery types and trace their evolution over a 400-600 year period. I seriously question some of the basic assumptions made in these pottery seriations. Just how reliable they are for chronological interpretations is, in my mind, open to question.

The Mitchell site permits the American Bottoms investigator an opportunity to study the types of structures, mounds and associated artifacts as they appeared while contemporary to a part of the "classic times" at Cahokia proper.

The Mitchell Site
Granite City, Illinois

The Mitchell site* is located on the floodplain of the Mississippi River, seven air miles north-northwest of Monks Mound (Fig. 1, 57). It derives its name from the small community of Mitchell, Illinois, through which Federal Interstate Highway 270 now passes. The site was excavated under the Highway Salvage Program in 1960, 1961, and 1962. The concentration of mounds and broken artifacts that constituted the site were located along the shore of Long Lake, a stagnant body of water in an ancient channel of the Mississippi River. The west end of the site was well-defined by the main channel of the Mississippi, abandoned most probably after Indian occupation. Although now some miles from the present river channel, it seems reasonable that at the time of occupation, the Mississippi flowed past the west end of the site and that Long Lake was a more active channel which diverted, like a bypass, to the southeast and "downtown" Cahokia.

The site was mapped by Bushnell on March 13, 1900 and reported in 1904 (Bushnell, 1904: 17). Although there is an error in his placement of Mound E, the site was essentially the same in 1960 as when it was first surveyed. In 1960 ten of the original eleven mounds could be identified. All had been heavily plowed for farming purposes and presented a rounded appearance. A large burial mound along the west side of the site (overlooking the main channel) was destroyed sometime in 1877 during the construction of railroads which still occupy the area (Fig. 57). So far as we can presently determine, the site covered between 80 and 100 acres. It may be larger if one could be certain of the actual limits, but modern urban expansion has dotted the area with roads, houses, businesses, schools and industry.

---

*SIU Site number 20B2-3, IAS number Ms-30.

Fig. 58. An aerial photo of the Mitchell site. The mounds are shown in the left center portion of the picture. Long Lake is the diagonal line running from the left center to the lower right hand portion of the picture.

The salvage excavations made it possible to test both sides of Long Lake and allowed at least a glimpse into eight of the ten mounds that remained in 1960. Only two mounds remain today and these may be removed within the next five years. The nature of the salvage operations can be viewed in two ways. For many purposes of data collection the salvage conditions left much to be desired, since it was excavated under constant highway construction pressure. Yet we can also note that this forced us to attempt getting as much of the site as possible, and like other salvage projects in the Cahokia region, we have turned our attention from small "test square" archaeology to a broad view of villages, towns, mounds, and other types of cultural manifestations.

Mounds

Although a more detailed discussion of one mound is required for my purposes, there are some general comments that can be offered on the basis of investigating eight of them. Not all mounds fit the description of platform mounds. Two of the smaller rounded mounds contained what might be described as stockpiles of soils for mound construction. They are labeled L and K on the map (Fig. 57). The smaller mounds B, H, and I paralleling Long Lake provided clear evidence of earlier structures beneath with some type of structure on top. In contrast, the larger mounds (C, E, A) appear to have no earlier buildings beneath and were built in a single construction period. The larger mounds are usually three times the size of the smaller ones, yet show no evidence of earlier building stages. One conclusion about the mounds at the site seems clear—they served different functions within the life of the site.

Town Square

Early in the excavation program it was speculated that four of the mounds might be thought of as defining a public square or plaza. Because of the way in which this site had to be excavated, we were finally able to test this hypothesis in 1961. In our letter assignments to mounds we find that the "town square" is defined by mounds H, C, A, and E (equals G, B, D, and E of Bushnell, 1904). The area was noticeably lacking in pottery and the evidence of houses or public structures.

In the central part of the plaza was located the largest post-pit found to date in the Cahokia region. Besides assisting in assigning a functional identification of "post-pit" to these features (which were previously known under various labels such as "bathtubs"), this pit produced one fascinating artifact. The base of a large bald-cypress log was found in the bottom, still leaning to the east where it had been left after it had broken during removal operations (Figs. 59, 60). This portion of the log, which is interpreted as being the central pole for the town, measured ten feet long and three and one-half feet in diameter at the base. I will later refer to radiocarbon analysis which has been completed for this specimen.

Living Units

In the excavation, we defined a number of scattered living units, with the types of artifacts one would expect to find associated with houses in which families dwelled. One of the advantages of the excavation at Mitchell is that we were not burdened with too many artifacts and repeated disturbances due to prehistoric activity. The houses were widely distributed (with some apparent plan) and no one set of superimposed dwellings was so complex that the sequence of buildings could not be determined. It was nearly impossible to define house floors, but the wall trenches were clear in the base clay. The pottery and other artifacts could therefore be positively associated with a given house or set of houses.

Fig. 59. This is the post pit excavated in the central portions of the Plaza at the Mitchell site. The remains of the log pole can be seen in the right central portion of the picture near the workman's hat.

Fig. 60. The bald cypress log that was removed from the post pit at the Mitchell site. The log was 10 feet in length and 3.5 feet in diameter.

For my purposes here I have chosen to set down some of the details on the feature 2 area and the feature 28-36 area.

The Features 28-36 Area: This unit consists of four superimposed dwellings. These were typical house patterns for the Cahokia region, being the outlines of wall trenches preserved in the base clay. The two earlier buildings measured approximately 6 x 3 meters, while the two larger had width measurements of 3.75 and 4.85 meters. The lengths of the two larger houses are unknown as they were not completely excavated. The orientations were all identical and a good sample of pottery was obtained from this area. There is no question that the pottery recovered comes from the occupations of these dwellings. Seventy percent of the pottery were jars, 28% bowls, and the remainder were beaker types. No plate rims were found. Six of the jars have broad incised lines and would be called Ramey Incised by those following Griffin's identifications (Griffin, 1949: 50). Different forms of Ramey designs are present on these six, one being a fine example of the curved ladder design. A few duck head effigies found would be listed with the bowl category as would the tail tabs from the same vessels. A few of the grog-tempered bowls would be classed as a "foreign type," having incised lines around the rim area as well as a distinctive groove along the top of the rim. These rims are suggestive of what to the south is called Coles Creek Incised.

In studying the feature 28 area pottery, the variety of jars and bowls (in terms of shapes and decoration) is surprising. The quantity of artifactual data, parallel alignment of the superimposed houses, and increase in size are presently viewed as representative of some family unit which either specializes in making pottery and/or accumulates enough wealth to own such a variety of it.

The Feature 2 Area: This is much less complex than the feature 28 area. There were two structures placed side by side, feature 2A measured 9 x 5.3 meters, while 2B measured approximately 6 x 2.8 meters. Feature 2B was parallel to 2A and was set in a scooped-out shallow rectangular basin. In terms of vessel shapes we have approximately 70% as jars, 28% as bowls, and the remainder are beakers. As with the feature 28 area, 80-90% are shell tempered with the others being grog-tempered. There is little difference in pottery between features 2A and 2B. A distinctively foreign bowl type was present. It has a scalloped flange and a very fine incised design in a small band along the rim. Looking for comparisons to the south has not yet been as fruitful as had been hoped. For this unique vessel type (three others have been found at the site) I have by chance noted an identical form in a short report on Ecuadorian pottery (Stirling and Stirling, 1963: PL. 6a). By no means do I suggest "trade" with South America, I merely find that for clear photographs of vessels similar in form to the vessels found in living units at Mitchell, one might refer to Stirling's Plate 6a.

The feature 2 area was on the level ground west of the south flank of Mound C. Feature 28 was as far north of feature 2 as it was possible to excavate under the salvage plans. They were approximately 235 meters (770 feet) apart. As in the case of many buildings at the site, they have alignments slightly east of north.

Cahokia Cordmarked pottery interests some colleagues working in the American Bottoms. The lack of this pottery type in our records for the feature 28 and 2 areas prompted a check of those instances where it was found at the site. Using our edge-punch cards (for rim sherds) and the program developed by Dr. Warren L. Wittry for the Illinois State Museum, we separated 8 cards which were Cahokia Cordmarked. Two of these came from areas south of Long Lake at what in the records is called the Fill site (a part of the Mitchell site). Of the remaining 6, one came from Mound H. It was recovered from a pit which would be associated with the structure placed on top. Another sherd came from the top of Mound C. One was found as part of the fill over a structure under the flanks of Mound B. The last three sherds were associated with Mound E. Except for the 2 found at the Fill site, all of the Cahokia Cordmarked sherds were found to be associated with the mounds H, C, B, and E.

Mound H

Much of my evidence for a short time period at the Mitchell site rests on the details of the building sequence beneath Mound H, which, according to my interpretation, flanks the town square. As a result of careful excavation of this mound I have encountered problems in interpreting the site using my colleagues' views of local chronology.

The mound contained evidence of a large structure being placed on top. Beneath the mound, which was constructed almost entirely of yellow brown silt (no cultural debris), was a set of three buildings. Each was distinct and the order of buildings was clearly visible where wall trenches crossed (Fig. 61). The earliest of these underlying structures was labeled feature 47 and measured 11 meters square (1296 square feet). It contained one large post pit with the deepest part in the center of the structure for placement of the central pole. A doorway faced east and a line of post holes, running from the east wall to the central pole, suggests a screen creating a kind of interior room. The large central post-pit was assigned the feature number 54.

Next in time was a larger building, feature 56. It measured 13.5 x 13.8 meters (2012.0 square feet), had a central post-pit and a doorway to the east. Following feature 56, the inhabitants built another building (after removing feature 56) and this we labeled feature 55. It measured 10 meters square (1075.8 square feet). After feature 55 was removed, they erected the mound

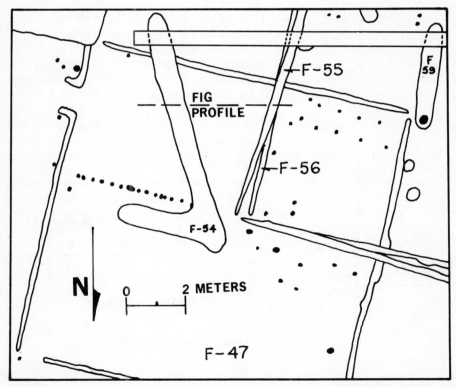

Fig. 61. A map of the feature 47 area. Underneath Mound H at the Mitchell site.

over the area. Feature 55 had to be demolished and in the profiles one could clearly see prehistoric diggings from the wall trenches and pits lying on the old humus, as if they had been left there only yesterday. The mound was then constructed in one stage over this set of superimposed structures, thereby sealing it off until the 1961 excavation. An earlier and smaller disturbance than ours is attributed to Warren K. Moorehead who ran an exploratory trench into the south side of the mound in March, 1923.

The key to interpretation in the mound H area was the position of the yellow-brown silt in relation to the above mentioned features. Each of the large structures (47, 56 and 55) had one large post-pit with the deepest portion in the center. The post-pit for feature 47 (earliest building) had been dug through the south wall trench and it was clear in plan view that the yellow-brown clay which filled the post holes was there because the wall posts had been removed. The south wall of feature 47 had been torn down so that the central post could be removed via the long arm of the post-pit. These events took place at the same time. Following this, the next building (56) was constructed and then removed in order to build feature 55. With the removal of feature 55, the yellow-brown silt was laid directly over the sequence to begin mound construction. What is most important is that in a number of profiles crossing the long arm of feature 54, one found definite evidence that water laid yellow-brown silt had washed off the mound surface and deposited in a shallow depression caused by the *still* sinking fill of feature 54 (Fig. 62).

In the deeper portions of the long arm of the post-pit this evidence was very noticeable and could be traced horizontally onto the mound from which it originated. The water deposited silt (rain wash) was not disturbed or found

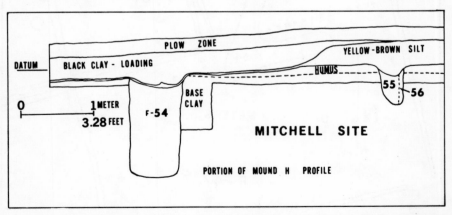

Fig. 62. A profile of a section of the excavation of Mound H showing the location of features 54, 55, and 56.

to cover any soil condition that one would naturally expect it to if this sequence had been exposed to the elements for any prolonged period (such as 5 years for each structure).

The interpretation of this sequence of buildings is that it represents a fourth stage of this series. I feel that it is more than coincidence, as well, that in the dwelling areas such as feature 28, we found no more than 4 sets of superimposed houses. The lack of fire basins in structures at the site might also be cited as support for a view that this is a seasonal occupation. Of further interest in connection with the mound H area is that other smaller buildings were found beneath the mound fill and these are most probably companion buildings to the large structures (47, 56 and 55). One was an 'L' shaped building like those found in "downtown" Cahokia by Warren L. Wittry. Another small set of three superimposed structures was also found. This set has as the earliest form a post hole type set in a shallow basin. The last two (with nearly identical orientations) were wall trench types (Fig. 63).

Fig. 63. Three superimposed structures underneath Mound H at the Mitchell site. The earliest of these is a pole type structure in a shallow pit. The later are the typical Mississippian wall trench type structures.

The orientations of this small set is approximately the same as the large buildings nearby. Those interested in the typology of dwelling types might easily develop a sequence from early to late for the variety—with the small early one a good representative of "Bluff" (Late Woodland) types. But the evidence found at Mitchell suggests that these are all structure types existing at essentially the same time, and serving different functions for the people of Mitchell.

Mound I

This small mound was approximately 150 meters southeast of Mound H and also along the edge of the slope to the shore of Long Lake. The physical proportions and yellow-brown silt fill suggested that one might be able to confirm the observation of a year earlier beneath mound H. All of the mound was lost in a few days due to salvage conditions, but thanks to the hard work of Alan Harn, Charles J. Bareis, Eugene Fugle, and Curtis Tunnell enough data were recovered to support those conclusions from data observed under mound H. Beneath mound I it was clear that there had been a series of superimposed structures very much like that found under mound H. Prominent were large post-pits, large structures, an 'L' shaped building, and small companion buildings. The 'L' shaped building was removed when the mound was built.

Carbon-14 Dating

Additional evidence for a short occupation at the Mitchell site can be taken from the results of radiocarbon dating. A number of samples have been dated and in all cases adequate amounts of material with meaningful provenience data had been submitted. Overall, the dates cluster rather tightly as noted by Fowler (1962: 49-57). Surprisingly, there were identical dates for three parts of the site: (a) burned structure on top of Mound B, (b) charred twigs from pit in the top of Mound C, and (c) charred wood from feature 28. All were dated at A.D. 1165±150. A pre-mound B structure was dated at A.D. 1075±150. The bald-cyress log produced a number of dates from various laboratories. Those from the Universities of Michigan, Texas, and Wisconsin are valid. Dates on the inner rings are A.D. 950, to which 100-120 years must be added since the samples submitted were from the center group of rings in a tree that, when cut, was approaching 300 years. By adding this factor, one arrives at a date of cutting circa A.D. 1050-1070. A run on the outer rings of A.D. 1050 (WIS-220) affirms this estimate remarkably (Bender, 1967).*

---

*In addition to the dates from the University of Wisconsin laboratory (WIS-220, 229) and those summarized by Fowler (1962), The *Institute Venezolano de Investigationes Cientificas* has published a date of A.D. 800 (IVIC-181) on the outer rings (*Radiocarbon*, Vol. 9, pp. 245).

Fowler's analysis of the dates suggested a narrow range of A.D. 1081-1195. For the general purpose of investigating the amount of time involved at the Mitchell Site, the radiocarbon results also suggest that, in general, it represents a short occupation.

Mitchell Site and the American Bottoms

Mitchell lies about halfway between the north bluffs of limestone at Alton, Illinois and Monks Mound in downtown Cahokia (Fig. 1). It occupies a key position for control over the confluence region of the Mississippi, Missouri, and Illinois Rivers. In addition, it has a natural "pipeline," or shortcut, to Cahokia via Long Lake. The success of the Mitchell site, as shortlived as it may have been, might well be tied directly to its position along the main channel. It may also be noted that most of the larger "Mississippian" sites in the American Bottoms are located along the junction of the prehistoric main channel with some major tributary (usually an earlier abandoned channel as in the case of Long Lake, an old oxbow).

In the Monks Mound area one sees a concentration of at least 100-120 mounds according to the latest computations of Fowler and Reed. There is a definite pattern to the central group very much like Mitchell. The early Patrick map clearly shows mounds all along the old channel of the Mississippi River, well down into present East St. Louis. Another instance of this pattern occurs in the vicinity of Dupo, Illinois—more specifically the Lunsford-Pulcher site (formerly called the Pulcher site). This pattern is still well preserved at the Lunsford-Pulcher site where the town square remains to be defined (if present at all). Until more substantial evidence can be brought to light, I prefer to attribute this difference in the three large sites to their location in rich bottomland and to economic factors of the period around A.D. 1000. Most investigators appear to favor a temporal factor, which is to a small degree true, but the Mitchell site, lying closer to the main urban center, shares more of the wealth of Cahokia than does Lunsford-Pulcher (Fig. 1). One can see the same thing today in contemporary cities in Manitoba. I could easily arrange the present cities of Altona, Brandon and Winnipeg into a series, in that order, and equate them to late Bluff, Old Village and Trappist. The labels used certainly designate differences, but it does not necessarily have to represent differences in time (at least not great differences). It is easy to see why this is inaccurate in Manitoba today and the problem is to determine if the situation in the American Bottoms around A.D. 1000 was not one of similar magnitude.

In order to properly interpret the Mitchell site, it would seem necessary to construct some model of the possible economic situation as it existed in the American Bottoms. It will be important to know the degree of interaction between contemporary "farmers," small villages, and centers.

The work on Monks Mound since 1964 has suggested that the earlier interior stages of the mound are massive, being major additions and representing that time when mounds were arranged parallel to the adjacent abandoned Mississippi River channel. In its later stages Monks Mound receives the attention of many rebuildings and the erection of large posts and buildings. Recently data has been published which suggests that Monks Mound was built in a relatively short time period (A.D. 900-1150) (Reed, Bennett, and Porter, 1968). This puts Mitchell in the last half of the Monks Mound construction range if one accepts my view of A.D. 1050-1150 for the Mitchell occupation.

There seems to be little question that Mitchell is contemporaneous with part of the "golden age" around Monks Mound in downtown Cahokia. When the "town square" idea arrives at Mitchell, it comes in literally overnight. Most probably this begins somewhat earlier in Cahokia. Using the dates from Monks Mound, I would guess that this structural feature develops around A.D. 1050±100 in the downtown area, while at Mitchell it is definitely in by A.D. 1150 if not A.D. 1100.

Midwestern View

Polanyi (1953: 173) has pointed out that his ". . . forms of integration do not represent 'stages' of development." He suggests that earlier "centers of civilization" could well have developed under the redistributive system economy. On this point I disagree and suggest that centers such as Cahokia could only develop with the assistance of a market type exchange system, regardless of how simple it might have been. For the present purposes I prefer to utilize an evolutionary scheme which involves the ever increasing complexity of the exchange systems. In what follows I will apply an evolutionary scheme to the general outline of Midwestern archaeological cultural periods.

The Archaic cultures appear to represent small groups who, as they gradually settle to a full exploitation of successively smaller and smaller areas, also continue to grow in numbers. It is here that I see reciprocity as the main system through which goods are exchanged outside their own territory. Lithic materials, for example, from foreign areas found in excavated sites are probably not representative of long range trade routes, but rather the products of reciprocal situations between neighboring Archaic groups.

We next look to Woodland cultures and their experimentation with pottery.

The Early Woodland cultures have been properly viewed as Archaic with the addition of pottery. Because of the emphasis placed on pottery as a tangible manifestation of culture, we are prone to assume that some major event attends the introduction of pottery. It would be tempting to see the beginnings of the redistribution system being developed in the Early Woodland cultures.

The classic Middle Woodland and its Hopewellian Interaction Sphere could easily be viewed as the continuation of the distributative system developed during Early Woodland times. For a good summary of this period one might consult Fowler's (1966: 3-6) paper. I do not agree entirely with his emphasis on the burial cult as a main feature of the Middle Woodland. It is true that great earthworks and burials with exotic materials attract our attention as prime criterion for delimiting this period, but this does not help to explain how it all came about. I would suggest that things such as the rich burials only reflect the success of the redistribution system. Certain individuals within the society have obviously amassed wealth in one form or another (along with status). I would further suggest that there is a good case in some Hopewell situations for the existence of Nash's mobilization type of system, which I have previously argued is only a special form of the redistribution system.

The goods and services are becoming centralized and the resulting earthworks, rich burials, and evidence of far-flung trade all point to a redistribution system with a social system involving various classes of people. For the Havana and Pike traditions (Illinois), Fowler (1966: 4-5) has noted that there are burial mound groups in clusters without any large earthworks as found in the Ohio Valley. He also cites Struever's work at Apple Creek as furthering our knowledge of the plants and water life exploited in the local environment.

I have studied some of Struever's ceramics with the petrographic microscope and can briefly summarize various highlights. His earlier pottery shows identical paste and temper features which make it difficult to separate the individual thin sections if they are not numbered. After we move into the area of the "classic" Hopewell pottery we find that the general local ware still shows an amazing similarity to earlier pottery although some shift in tempering practice is noted. Along with this local ware are some of the distinctive Hopewell ceramic types. They, in contrast, provide a wide variety of differences in paste features, types of temper, and quantity of temper. One gets the feeling that no one of the vessels was made in the same family tradition. If this, after more analysis of thin sections, is borne out for the whole sequence, I can see that redistribution is bringing in more and more materials from further and further afield. This would fit a view that population had expanded by this time and that there were possible contacts with the more complex cultures of Mesoamerica.

As we move into the Late Woodland period in the Cahokia region, we find colleagues referring to it as a period of "cultural decline." I fail to see any value in this view since it can only mean that people stopped building earthworks and burying Indians the way we might like. I do not doubt that most of our so-called Late Woodland people (Bluff culture around Cahokia) are an outgrowth of the Middle Woodland. This may well be in terms of biological and overall cultural traits, but I would add to this that by A.D. 700-900 these people are feeling the impact of economic developments going on in the Mesoamerican region. Looking southward I feel we will find the evidence at this time of developing redistribution systems along with the beginning of the market system. Using the Mississippi River as a north-south line I visualize an ellipsoid of diffusion for these ideas stemming from the development of ports of trade along the river. Even if developed in a few places, the impact could well be felt as far north as St. Louis by A.D. 900.

The key to "Mississippian" problems around Cahokia may well rest on how well we understand these Late Woodland-Bluff cultures. I have had a tendency to view them much as Nash has classed some of the more remote tribes of modern Mexico. These people, like others in Mexico today are still the delight of anthropological study. They are in part tied to a modern market system, yet display a variety of features that would suggest they are still putting some emphasis on older practices. Our Late Woodland people might very well be viewed as the product of varying degrees of acculturation all along the length of the Mississippi River. These American Bottoms Woodland peoples have been partially studied by Munson (1966) in his survey of a part of the bottoms. We know that they were exploiting clays and temper from the bluff areas and that these products are found widely scattered over the floodplain. Munson has, in part, documented their seasonal movements and population growth through time. They appear to rapidly gain in numbers as they slowly shift their emphasis to lowland areas where one can speculate that farming is of some importance. One point that has disturbed me is why they should do so? It is easy to say that they did, but I prefer to see them doing so in response to pressures from the Cahokian community to produce food. Unless farming provides some major cultural benefit, I fail to see them practicing farming for the "fun of it." Becoming farmers is not that easy, since much of the culture must change when shifting from a hunting and gathering background. We need only remind ourselves of the pains and abuses of Indians during the early history of the U.S.A. which refused to accord any real humanity to "those lazy people who can't grow corn." Even if some Late Woodland peoples *did* rapidly become farmers (in the sense of settled tillers/ tenders of the soil) I doubt that all of the "hinterland" people did so. Those who would cite the meager evidence of "farming" in Middle Woodland times might give thought to that evidence as representing part of a unique redistributive system which allows the developing power at the center to trade for corn grown experimentally some distance away. In this situation the corn has to come from the south.

In connection with my views on Late Woodland-Bluff cultures I have again retreated to historical data which I feel sheds light on the problems of interpretation. In this case I am particularly interested in a paper by Wright (1967). In his presentation of relevant historical data regarding early "exchange networks" in the Great Lakes region, he notes:

> The historical data . . . indicates that foodstuffs was one of the major classes of items being exchanged across these ecological (and ethnic) boundaries. In particular, maize, beans, sunflower seeds, and oil were traded out of the agricultural area . . . into the Canadian and Hudsonian provinces, which had little or no agricultural protential. . . .Meat and fish were the major food items received in exchange from the hunting bands. (Wright, 1967: 185)

His use of ecological factors to explain what takes place in trade over a wide region is the type of approach which will shed light on the history of the Cahokian community. Besides foodstuffs flowing in an exchange system, other materials he lists include: tobacco, manufactured reed mats, hemp, squash, medicinal herbs, hunting and traveling equipment, moose skins, and furs. Seldom is there mention of chert, copper, shell, ceramics, and pigments. In contemplating this list, it is an almost perfect division of materials into those found in archaeological contexts (preserved) and those seldom found (only traces—materials generally utilized or decayed).

Another impressive factor brought out by Wright is the *amount* of material moved and the *distances* involved. These historic tribes were certainly, in part, related to the earlier "Mississippian" and, when observed in the earliest periods, would hardly create a picture of the majestic savage.

In any case, around Cahokia, by Late Woodland times, we find a people who live part of the year on the upper prairies using post-hole house types, pottery tempered with grit and grog, and using shales for clays when in the bluff area. When exploiting the bottomlands they shift their attention to bottomland clays, utilize rectangular pits, and exploited local game and vegetation. Munson (1966) has contributed some information to this view here through his comments regarding the Late Woodland picture based on his surface survey. Munson concludes: "Considerable evidence of trade exists in the Bluff contexts, although the emphasis had shifted from that of the preceding Middle Woodland " (Munson, 1966: 28). He mentions that the types of chert include Dongola chert, Crescent Quarry, Mill Creek, and an "unclassified glossy, dark blue-grey, slightly fossiliferous chert." This last type sounds very much like a type common in the Chester, Illinois, region where the outcrop distribution is fairly well restricted (15 mile belt along the Mississippi River bluffs on the Illinois side). This, the Dongola, and the Mill Creek chert point to the south for these materials. When I indicate southern sources in this case it is well within a 200 mile distance, yet southern for the most part. In addition Munson has noted the presence of material such as copper and marginella shell which suggest contacts from even further afield. These are tempting, but being small in the artifactual assemblage as compared to other non-perishables which survive tests of time, we tend to see these few bits of material as evidence of weak outside influences. If the analogy with Wright's data is worth anything at all, I would suggest this only represents what we might expect where people may be moving greater quantities of materials and manufactured goods which are perishable or consumed by the prehistoric individuals.

In the time period A.D. 700-900 we see the development of settlements in the bottomlands, which Fowler (1966: 9) has pointed to as "complex temple-town type of settlement." He has recognized a settlement pattern that involves a main ceremonial center which functions as the political center of a large population. It contains temple mounds, plazas, and other public buildings. Nearby are found smaller towns which contain few mounds and a single plaza. In all of these more elaborate towns and centers we would expect a local populace and their resultant debris. Further afield one could visualize the spread of farmsteads or what is identical to our early historic farmers through the Midwest—exploiting a particular small section of land with the family as the primary production unit. Fowler's (1966: 7-8) view provides a realistic base for my own interests and is based on archaeological evidence from the whole American Bottoms. Further elaboration of Fowler's view might be made with the help of the Mitchell site data. During the beginning of his introduction of "Mississippian" from elsewhere, an early phase in the development of a large political center would be seen at Mitchell. When looking over the American Bottoms, those familiar with it can point to lines of mounds that run from the Dupo area, through Cahokia proper, and up to Mitchell. I suggest that the Late Woodland people were beginning to profit from the results to the south and were participating in a system of exchange with which they were already familiar. Meeting along the main highway for the region (Mississippi River) and exchanging goods with "southern" traders is not too remote a possibility. This would be better seen as some variety of the redistributive system, and the mounds would represent the center for more and more groups. One might think of this as a continuation and/or revival of Middle Woodland practices. It may well be that the elaborate burials (see Fowler, this volume) in some of the mounds are a result of this type of phenomenon, one that owes its Hopewellian similarities to the same type of economic exchange system.

Around A.D.1000, I believe that the work of traders from the south imparted an impact when accompanied by movements of people into a relatively rich area. This timing is not out of line with developments going on in the Mexican highlands at this time. In connection with this aspect of my speculations I found Anne M. Chapman's (1957: 114-153) paper very useful. She clearly records the importance, the characteristics, and the fate of long distance trade in Aztec and Maya civilizations. Abstracting from a wealth of early documents and ethnographic literature she has provided a highly suggestive frame of reference for Cahokian research.

The trader was certainly a reality by Aztec times and an important figure in the ultimate success of the Middle American urban centers. Besides Chapman's discussion of the traders and their roles in the society, she outlines the details of specific locations which functioned as "ports of trade." Polanyi (1953: 176), as well, describes the port of trade as "the specialized organ of administered trade." The ports of trade described by the early Spanish seem to have prospered and only fell to lesser status with the impact of Old World conquest. It is in these ports of trade that large regional governments (through their traders) can carry on some type of trade.

In so far as Cahokian speculations are concerned I found Chapman's discussion of particular interest in the area of the trader. She points to the *pochteca* as the long distance traders for the Aztec sphere. From the earlier literature it is clear that the *pochteca* were socially ranked into four or five classes. One of these, the slave traders, appear to have maintained high status and dealt with the importation of slaves. For the complexity of Middle American prehistoric societies I see the source of labor needed to build and maintain such impressive monuments and centers as Teotihuacan. Rene Millon (1964; 1967) has clearly portrayed Teotihuacan as a magnificent center with a wide variety of people entering into its principle achievements. Millon (personal communication, summer 1968) has also pointed out some of the latest result of his research which suggests that traders (or something similar) were occupying particular areas of the great site at the same time (see also Parsons, 1968).

Thought is seldom given to the meaning of Cahokia in terms of slave labor but the impressive size of Cahokia and the volume of earth moved (not to mention the other evidence of energy expenditure) suggest it would be difficult to achieve even under some "mystical" religious coercion and the redistributive system of exchange. The Cahokia center and its satellite communities should be viewed much as one might view Teotihuacan or a similar site from prehistory. The redistributive system contains what is needed to see the next stage of complexity—the market exchange system. In this case we are speaking of the market as a place where sellers and buyers interact. We have the historic literature to assure us that this was truly the case when the

Spanish intruded. Why should Cahokia be left out of the picture? Its geographic location is certainly no hindrance.

When looking at the *pochteca,* a list of the imported items is interesting. It includes such items as feathers, precious stones, gold, animal skins, and other *raw* materials. This is in some respects reminiscent of Wright's views for the historic situation in the Great Lakes. These great centers contained the craft specialists from whom finished products could be exported. Although markets were present, these *pochteca* (except in a few instances) did not operate through the market system. They developed and maintained ports of trade. I found it interesting to have a record of what one could call a typical caravan. Not only are leading *pochteca* present, but porters as well. It is clear that these trips were not generally single individual efforts journeying across country but were regular supply trains like our modern trucking companies and their regularly spaced cross-country units. If Cahokia were to be participating with caravans of this sort, there is no question that there were people coming into Cahokia in goodly numbers. In addition, they could quickly settle to develop this center for their own purposes. In this way they could have formed a port of trade, never completely losing contact with their cultural homeland.

A view of Cahokia as a port of trade is not too impossible. Chapman (1957: 115) says: "The word 'port' as employed here, need not imply a coastal or riverain site, *although ports of trade were usually thus situated* " (italic mine).

In Cahokia around A.D. 1000, many new items come into prominence. As at Mitchell, it seems as if the concept of the "Town Square" appears overnight. I would prefer that this development of the town square be considered as the development of the actual *market place* for the beginnning of a market exchange system. This view does not mean that redistribution systems are immediately scrapped. It suggests that as an outgrowth of long time redistribution experience and the increased flow of ideas from the south, the market place itself begins to develop.

Around A.D. 1000 there seems to be general agreement that a large population is living in and around Monks Mound. When characterizing the Cahokia site, archaeologists have emphasized Monks Mound. Impressive as this "Pyramid of the Sun" may be, what is more impressive is the number of other large mounds arranged in some kind of patttern, the stockades (James Anderson's work around Monks Mound), and the tremendous amount of energy that was utilized in rebuilding structures. I believe no one sees this as a result of employing the basics of reciprocity. Most might see a complex redistribution system being adequate to develop such centers as Cahokia. I fail to see the spark needed in such systems. I suggest that a market system actually developed in and around Cahokia by A.D. 1100 when "town squares" appear. The area had the necessary population, and market systems were already established in Mesoamerica.

These town squares are the market places in my view and could have served for religious functions as well. There is no question that religious support of the exchange systems is necessary. I find archaeological dependence upon ceremonialism as an explanation of phenomena highly unrealistic. We are wearing out the hinges on the "back door" of ceremonialism. The issues are more or less evaded when faced with the tremendous archaeological complexity of Cahokia and related satellite communities. In the ceremonialism sphere, I would mention in passing that certain key items which are used to tie together the so-called Mississippian over great geographic areas may well be the movement of international traders under a system of reciprocity. As has been pointed out by Polanyi and Nash, we will find all three types of exchange systems operating side-by-side to some extent.

The Cahokians can also be seen to be interacting closely with local Late Woodland types. If we return to Nash's Middle American examples of various areas interacting with the modern market system, one could visualize another dynamic situation in which our Late Woodland peoples are moving from a redistributive system to the market type. One thing is clear and that is that the Spanish found a complex market system in operation and from a light perusal of the descriptions, via other authors, it appears to have time depth, at least back to Teotihuacan times. The better question would be: how far afield would one see the effects of this well developed system? I would guess that Cahokia itself is ample testimonial for "how far."

Employing my view of the economic exchange systems as they might have existed at Cahokia, I now desire to select items from colleagues' writings regarding Cahokia and view the data in terms of my hypothetical picture.

Warren L. Wittry has presented a picture of great circles of posts erected, possibly, for calendrical purposes (see this volume). The obvious feature of these great circles involves the amount of energy needed to erect such projects. The use of calendrical devices on the part of agricultural peoples is not in itself astounding, but where would we search for anything in the New World that resembles this type of feature? My belief is that we must look southward, and at the same time, be prepared to accept the possibility that direct long distance movements are responsible for their conception. The use of the post-pit principle in the erection of large posts force me to restudy the Mitchell site data to see if there was any suggestion of an earlier phase in which the post-pit was not used in large structures. On the west side of the site we had excavated a large double wall trench structure that did not contain a post-pit. It was so located that it would fit my interpretation of the earlier phase of occupation in which there are a string of large structures paralleling the lake shore. If our feature 7 belongs to this phase, then, we can, by going back to the evidence under mound H, say that the post-pit idea comes in overnight as well.

Many prefer to see ceremonialism in connection with these large circles or any free standing "central" pole. It is true that we might lose a few "virgins" now and then around the pole, but I would rather see these also connected in some way to the exchange system.

Fowler (1966: 9) in discussing regions in the north, away from Cahokia, mentions that around A.D. 1200 "there is a re-adaptation of the subsistence pattern" to "mixed bison hunting and agriculture." I would like to proceed from that point and suggest something in addition. Granted that climatic shifts might have some major effect on the agricultural productivity of the Cahokia region, more interesting might be the speculation on what this shift means in terms of evolving economic systems.

In view of Wright's paper (1967), we need not emphasize climatic change in the immediate Cahokia region, but merely point to its great hinterland area where a climatic change would rapidly shift ecological boundaries. This, in turn, would affect the center more than any other place if the center has been depending upon these areas for a substantial portion of its subsistence material. I believe that these hinterland people were not so rapidly converted to market ways and that they were always hunters as well as "experimentalists" with corn. There is no direct way of determining how they procured the corn cobs which have been excavated. They may have served, for some time, as the outlying source for basic resources for a complex market center (Cahokia). This would only be an extension of Wright's views of the early historic period in the Great Lakes region. The people from adjacent regions would continue to maintain much of the redistributive system for exchange of their local products in their own regions, but participate in the market system to the southeast just as in Nash's adjunct export system.

If anything happened to the main center, as it most certainly did, these outlying people would have little trouble re-adjusting or re-adapting. They probably had a great amount of meat to eat for awhile, but in time they would readjust to a system that was already present and well understood. In this case I do not need missionaries or great religious movements to explain the presence of a number of "Mississippian" traits, I only require some contact and a system that allows me to convey goods over a long distance. Because Cahokia is centrally located in the continent, it is not surprising to see the "Mississippian" influence over a wide area on all sides.

Literature concerning long distance traders in Aztec times has presented pictures that at first seem impossible to believe. But archaeological evidence continues to demonstrate that this type of movement was not new. Cahokia, as a major market center (in its simpler form), is all that is needed to explain a great deal of the "Mississippian problem." When the center "died" so went changes at the edges of the sphere. A few features continue, allowing some historical connection to be intimated. For example, the use of shell tempering continues on into later periods. What is more interesting is that, in some cases, there are shell and grit tempered wares in contemporary contexts. This dichotomy exists in Cahokia, for whatever reasons (seasonal?) and continues into recent times.

Since I have mentioned changes at the edge of the sphere as due to problems at the center, it would be worthwhile to note that these changes need not be the same magnitude or contemporaneous all around the sphere. The ideas and the trade are flowing in from the south, and to the north we would expect the "frontier" where life and encounters with hostiles would be a distinct feature. It should be in the north that we also see the first signs of shifts (for whatever reason). To the south we could expect that the "Mississippian" way (e.g., the Natchez?) continued for some time.

In looking to the north, the first site that impresses one is Aztalan. This site in southern Wisconsin is an example of "frontier life" connected to the evolving exchange system to the south at Cahokia. This site had direct ties with Cahokia. In a recent paper I pointed out some of the resemblances in the microscopic features of pottery temper and the use of local clays (Porter, 1966). This site's palisade also suggests problems with the local "natives." If one counts the number of posts in the sections of reconstructed stockade and surveys the site from the top of the two large platform mounds, one envisions a great deal of energy having been expended. As a frontier outpost (perhaps, for the developing copper trade?) it is easy to note the developing market exchange system affecting local situations. The presence of cherts from Cahokia clearly signals connections between Cahokia and Aztalan. Going in the other direction we might point to at least three microscopic identifications of Hixton Silicified Sediment (Porter, 1961) for that material in Cahokia. One is from the surface around Roach Mound (thin section T-21). The other two are from Charles J. Bareis' excavations at the airport site (S34-1) and south of Grandpa's Store (thin sections T-12 and T-13 of S34/9277 and S34/9097-University of Illinois catalogue). All are lighter varieties most common at the source.

When we see Aztalan's influence fading, it appears to topple rather violently. At least the economic picture might change quickly this far from the center. Here the natives could quickly revert to their simpler system of redistribution that was, most probably, still being practiced with the bulk of goods. The scene at Aztalan should focus attention back to Cahokia where recent excavations and use of aerial photographs by Fowler and Anderson (see this volume) have clearly demonstrated the presence of great sections of palisade around the core of the mound complex. This I would equate to a situation in which the entire exchange system is under pressure from the local natives. These "local natives" must be viewed as somewhat acculturated Late Woodland types that are further removed from the center and its "Mississippianized" natives. Since I see Mitchell as comparatively short-lived, I can also see Mitchell coming to a rather sudden end around A.D. 1150-1200. The great log was taken from the town square, breaking during the effort. The people practicing a market exchange system had grown as wealthy as possible under the conditions and the system was beginning to decay. The outlying hinterland to the north and west contained people who probably found the centers vulnerable during times of shortage. In these areas as well, there was never a complete conversion to the market system, only varying degrees of participation (as in Mexico today). Because of this situation, it is the hinterland area that experiences the end of "Mississippian" and the appearance of an economic situation resembling the Woodland types. I am suggesting that the end of the so-called "Mississippian" can be viewed in terms of the decay of the market system and a return to the simpler and more individualistic redistribution system—a system never entirely lacking in the practices of the Woodland people.

References Cited

Bender, Margaret M., Reid A. Bryson, and David A. Baerreis
    1968   University of Wisconsin Radiocarbon Dates IV, *Radiocarbon* 10: 161-168.

Bohannan, Paul and George Dalton
    1965   *Markets in Africa.* Anchor Books, New York.

Bushnell, David I.
    1904   The Cahokia and Surrounding Mound Groups. *Papers of the Peabody Museum of American Archaeology and Ethnology.* Vol. III, No. 1, pp. 5-20. Cambridge.

Chapman, Anne M.
    1957   Ports of Trade Enclaves in Aztec and Maya Civilizations. In: K. Polanyi, C. Arensber, and H. Pearson, *Trade and Market in The Early Empires.* pp. 114-153.

Dalton, George
    1968   Review of Nash's "Primitive and Peasant Economic Systems," *American Anthropologist.* Vol. 70, pp. 368-369. Menasha.

Fowler, Melvin L.
    1962   Radiocarbon Assays, In *First Annual Report: American Bottoms Archaeology.* Illinois Archaeological Survey, Urbana.

1966 Archicultural and Village Settlement in the North American East: The Central Mississippi Valley Area, A Case History, *XXXVI Congreso Internacional de Americanistas.* Vol. 1, pp. 229-240. Sevilla.

Gabel, Creighton
1967 *Analysis of Prehistoric Economic Patterns.* Holt, Reinhart and Winston, New York.

Gibson, Charles
1964 *The Aztecs Under Spanish Rule.* Stanford University Press, Stanford, California.

Griffin, James B.
1949 The Cahokia Ceramic Complexes. *Proceedings of the Fifth Plains Conference for Archaeology* (J. L. Champe, editor), The University of Nebraska. Lincoln.

Hall, Robert L.
1967a More About Corn, Cahokia and Carbon-14. *A Report of Research in Progress Prepared for Distribution at the Cahokia Field Conference,* August 5-6, 1967. Collinsville, Ill.
1967b Those Late Corn Dates: Isotopic Fractionation as a Source of Error in Carbon-14 Dates. *Michigan Archaeologist,* Vol. 13, No. 4, pp. 171-180. Ann Arbor.

Jennings, Jesse D.
1968 *Prehistory of North America.* McGraw-Hill Book Company, New York.

Millon, Rene
1964 The Teotihuacan Mapping Project. *American Antiquity,* Vol. 29, No. 3, pp. 345-352. Salt Lake City.
1967 "Teotihuacan. *Scientific American,* Vol. 216, No. 6, pp. 38-48. New York.

Munson, Patrick J.
1966 An Archaeological Survey of the 'Wood River Terrace' and Adjacent Bottoms and Bluffs in Madison County, Illinois. *Illinois State Museum Preliminary Reports,* No. 8. Springfield, Ill.

Nash, Manning
1966 *Primitive and Peasant Economic Systems.* Chandler Publishing Company, San Francisco.

Parsons, Jeffrey R.
1968 Teotihuacan, Mexico, and Its Impact on Regional Demography. *Science,* Vol. 162, #3856, pp. 872-877. Washington, D.C.

Polanyi, Karl, Conrad M. Arensber, and Harry W. Pearson
    1957   *Trade and Market in the Early Empires.* The Free Press
           Glencoe, Illinois.

Porter, James Warren
    1961   Hixton Silicified Sediment: A Unique Lithic Material Used by
           Prehistoric Cultures. *The Wisconsin Archeologist,* Vol. 42,
           No. 1, pp. 78-85. Milwaukee.
    1966   Thin Section Analysis of Ten Aztalan Sherds. *The Wisconsin
           Archeologist,* Vol. 47, No. 1, pp. 12-27, Milwaukee.

Reed, Nelson, A., John W. Bennett and James Warren Porter
    1968   Solid Core Drilling of Monks Mound. Technique and Find-
           ings. *American Antiquity,* Vol. 33, No. 2, pp. 137-148. Salt
           Lake City.

Soustelle, Jacques
    1964   *The Daily Life of the Aztecs.* Pelican Books, Great Britain.

Stirling, M. W. and M. Stirling
    1963   Tarqui, An Early Site in Manabi Province, Ecuador. *Anthro-
           pology Paper No. 63.* Bureau of American Ethnology Bulletin
           186, pp. 1-28. Washington, D.C.

Willey, Gordon R.
    1966   *An Introduction to American Archaeology: Volume I-North and
           Middle America.* Prentice-Hall, Inc., New Jersey.

Wright, Gary A.
    1967   Some Aspects of Early and Mid-Seventeenth Century
           Exchange Networks in the Western Great Lakes. *Michigan
           Archaeologist,* Vol. 13, No. 4, pp. 181-197. Ann Arbor.
    1968   A Further Note on Trade Friendship and Gift Giving in the
           Western Great Lakes. *Michigan Archaeologist,* Vol. 14, No.
           3-4, pp. 165-166. Ann Arbor.

BIBLIOGRAPHY

Anonymous

1820 *History of North America.* Vol. 2, Davies and Company, Leeds, England.

1873 *Illustrated Encyclopedia and Atlas Map of Madison County (Illinois).* Brink, St. Louis.

1888 The Monk's Mound: A Prehistoric Marvel in Madison County, Illinois. *St. Louis Daily Globe-Democrat,* February 5, p. 16. St. Louis.

1891 Archaeological Notes: The Patrick Collection. *The American Antiquarian,* Vol. 13, p. 245. Chicago.

1908 Cistercians in America. *Catholic Encyclopedia,* Vol. 3, p. 787. The Encyclopedia Press, Inc., New York.

1909 The Great Cahokia Mound to be Sold. *Journal of the Illinois State Historical Society,* Vol. 2 (No. 2), pp. 19-20. Springfield.

1931 Ancient Tumulus Leveled to Make Truck Farm Discloses Evidence of High Civilization. *St. Louis Post-Dispatch,* March 4, 1931. St. Louis.

Baker, Frank Collins

1924 The Use of Molluscan Shells by the Cahokia Mound Builders. *Transactions of the Illinois State Academy of Science,* Vol. 16, pp. 328-334. Springfield.

Bareis, Charles J.

1964 Meander Loops and the Cahokia Site. *American Antiquity,* Vol. 30 (No. 1), pp. 89-91. Salt Lake City.

1967 *Report on Preliminary Site Examination Undertaken at the Faust Site (S-69) on FAI 64, St. Clair County, Illinois.* Illinois Archaeological Survey. Urbana, Illinois. (Mimeographed)

1968 *Report of Salvage Work Undertaken at the Faust Site (S-69) on FAI 64, St. Clair County, Illinois.* Illinois Archaeological Survey. Urbana, Illinois. (Mimeographed)

Bareis, Charles J. and James Warren Porter

1965 Megascopic and Petrographic Analyses of a Foreign Pottery Vessel from the Cahokia Site. *American Antiquity,* Vol. 31 (No. 1), pp. 95-101. Salt Lake City.

Baum, Rev. Henry Mason

1903 Antiquities of the United States: The Cahokia Mounds. *Records of the Past.* Vol. 2, pp. 214-222. Washington, D.C.

Beck, Lewis C.

1823 *A Gazetteer of the States of Illinois and Missouri.* C. R. and G. Webster, Albany.

Brackenridge, Henry Marie
    1811   Unsigned article in *The Missouri Gazette,* January 9, 1811. St. Louis.
    1814   *Views of Louisiana together with a Journal of a Voyage up the Missouri River, in 1811.* Pittsburgh. (Modern edition published 1962 by Quadrangle Books, Inc., Chicago).
    1818a   On the Population and Tumuli of the Aborigines of North America. In a Letter from H.M. Brackenridge, Esq. to Thomas Jefferson—Read Oct. 1, 1813. *Transactions of the American Philosophical Society,* Vol. 1 (New Series) pp. 151-159. Philadelphia.
    1818b   On the Population and Tumuli of the Aborigines of North America. In a letter from H. M. Brackenridge, Esq. to Thomas Jefferson. *Analectic,* Vol. 11 (No. 7), pp. 326-331.

Bushnell, David I. Jr.
    1904   The Cahokia and Surrounding Mound Groups. *Papers of the Peabody Museum of American Archaeology and Ethnology (1904-1913),* Vol. 3 (No. 1), pp. 3-20. Harvard University, Cambridge.
    1917   The Origin and Various Types of Mounds in Eastern United States. *Proceedings Nineteenth International Congress of Americanists, Washington, 1915.* pp. 43-47. Washington.
    1922   Archaeological Reconnaissance of the Cahokia and Related Mound Groups. Explorations and Field Work of the Smithsonian Institution in 1921. *Smithsonian Miscellaneous Collections,* Vol. 72 (No. 15), pp. 92-105. Washington.

Carr, Lucian
    1893   The Mounds of the Mississippi Valley, Historically Considered. *Annual Report of the Board of Regents of the Smithsonian Institution, July, 1891,* pp. 503-605. Washington.

Conant, A. J.
    1879   *Foot-Prints of Vanished Races.* Chancy R. Barns, St. Louis.

Crook, A. R.
    1915   Origin of Monks Mound. *Bulletin of the Geological Society of America,* Vol. 26, pp. 74-75. New York.
    1916   The Composition and Origin of Monks Mound. *Transactions of the Illinois Academy of Science,* Vol. 9, pp. 82-84. Springfield.
    1918   Additional Note on Monks Mound. *Bulletin of the Geological Society of America,* Vol. 29, pp. 80-81. New York.
    1922   The Origin of the Cahokia Mounds. *Bulletin of the Illinois State Museum,* Springfield.

DeHass, W.
  1869   Archaeology of the Mississippi Valley. *Proceedings of the American Association for the Advancement of Science 17th Meeting held at Chicago, Illinois, August, 1868,* pp. 288-302. Joseph Lovering, Cambridge.

Dick, George C.
  1955   Incised Pottery Decorations from Cahokia. *The Missouri Archaeologist,* Vol. 17 (No. 4), pp. 36-48. Columbia, Mo.

English, Thomas H.
  1921   The Cahokia Indian Mounds: A Plea for their Preservation. *The Geographical Review,* Vol. 2 (No. 2), pp. 207-211. New York.

Featherstonhaugh, G. W.
  1844   *Excursion through the Slave States.* Vol. 1. Harper, London and New York.

Fecht, William G.
  1960   Cahokia Mounds Serpent Pottery. *Central States Archaeological Journal,* Vol. 7 (No. 1), pp. 34-35. Fayetteville.

Fenneman, N. M.
  1911   Geology and Mineral Resources of the St. Louis Quadrangle Missouri-Illinois. *U.S. Geological Survey Bulletin 438.* Department of the Interior, Washington.

Flagg, Edmund
  1838   *The Far West: or, A Tour Beyond the Mountains.* Vol. 1. Harper & Brothers, New York.

Flint, Timothy
  1826   *Recollections of The Last Ten Years, Passed in Occasional Residences and Journeyings in the Valley of the Mississippi, from Pittsburgh and the Missouri to the Gulf of Mexico, and from Florida to the Spanish Frontier; in a Series of Letters to the Rev. James Flint, of Salem, Massachusetts.* Cummings, Hilliard, and Company, Boston.

Fowke, Gerard
  1910   Antiquities of Central and Southeastern Missouri. *Bureau of American Ethnology,* Bulletin 37, pp. 5-7. Washington.

Fowler, Melvin L.
  1962   John Francis Snyder: Pioneer Illinois Archaeologist. In *John Francis Snyder: Selected Writings,* edited by Clyde C. Walton, pp. 181-273. Illinois State Historical Society, Springfield.

Fowler, Melvin L. (editor)
  1962   *First Annual Report: American Bottoms Archaeology, July 1, 1961–June 30, 1963.* Illinois Archaeological Survey, Urbana.

1963   *Second Annual Report: American Bottoms Archaeology, July 1, 1962–June 30, 1963.* Illinois Archaeological Survey, Urbana. (Mimeographed)

1964   *Third Annual Report: American Bottoms Archaeology, July 1, 1963–June 30, 1964.* Illinois Archaeological Survey, Urbana. (Mimeographed)

Garraghan, Gilbert J.

1934   *Chapters in Frontier History.* Bruce Publishing Company, Milwaukee.

Griffin, James B.

1941   Report on Pottery from the St. Louis Area. *The Missouri Archaeologist,* Vol. 7 (No. 2), pp. 1-17. Columbia, Mo.

1949   The Cahokia Ceramic Complexes. *Proceedings of the Fifth Plains Conference for Archaeology,* Vol. 1, pp. 44-57. Laboratory of Anthropology. University of Nebraska, Lincoln.

1960   A Hypothesis for the Prehistory of the Winnebago. In *Culture in History, Essays in Honor of Paul Radin,* edited by Stanley Diamond, pp. 852-862. Columbia University Press, New York.

Griffin, James B., and Albert C. Spaulding

1951   The Central Mississippi Valley Archaeological Survey, Season 1950–A Preliminary Report. *Journal of the Illinois State Archaeological Society,* (new series), Vol. 1 (No. 3), pp. 74-81. Fairbury, Illinois.

Grimm, R. E. (editor)

1949   *Cahokia Brought to Life: An Artifactual Story of America's Greatest Monument.* The Greater St. Louis Archaeological Society, Wellington Printing Co., St. Louis.

Hair, James T. (compiled and published by)

1866   *Gazetteer of Madison County.* S. V. Crossman and Company, Printers. Alton, Illinois.

Hall, Robert L.

1967   The Mississippian Heartland and Its Plains Relationship. *Plains Anthropologist,* Vol. 12 (No. 36), pp. 175-183. Lincoln.

1967   Northern Mississippi Valley. *American Antiquity,* Vol. 32 (No. 4), p. 571, Salt Lake City.

1968   The Goddard-Ramey Cahokia Flight: A Pioneering Aerial Photographic Survey. *The Wisconsin Archeologist,* Vol. 49 (No. 2), pp. 75-79. Milwaukee.

Holmes, William H.

1883   Art in Shell. *Transactions of the Anthropological Society of Washington,* Vol. 2, pp. 106-107. Washington.

1903 Aboriginal Pottery of the Eastern United States. *20th Annual Report of the Bureau of American Ethnology,* pp. 1-201. Washington.

Howland, Henry R.
1877 Recent Archaeological Discoveries in the American Bottom. *Buffalo Society of Natural Sciences Bulletin,* Vol. 3 (No. 5), pp. 204-211. Buffalo.

James, James Alton
1928 *The Life of George Rogers Clark.* University of Chicago Press, Chicago.

Judd, Neil M.
1948 'Pyramids' of the New World. *National Geographic Magazine,* Vol. 93, pp. 105-128. Washington.

Kelly, A. R.
1933 Some Problems of Recent Cahokia Archaeology. *Transactions of the Illinois State Academy of Science,* Vol. 25 (No. 4), pp. 101-103. Springfield.

Kelly, A.R., and Fay-Cooper Cole
1931 Rediscovering Illinois. *Blue Book of the State of Illinois 1931-1932,* pp. 328-334. Springfield.

Keplinger, John C.
1919 Who Were the Mound Builders? *Illinois State Historical Society Journal,* Vol. 12, pp. 45-52. Springfield.

Kirkpatrick, John Erwin
1911 *Timothy Flint, Pioneer, Missionary, Author, Editor 1780-1840: The Story of his life among the Pioneers and Frontiersmen in the Ohio and Mississippi Valley and in New England and the South.* The Arthur H. Clark Company, Cleveland.

Latrobe, Charles Joseph
1835 *The Rambler in North America,* Vol. 2, Harper & Brothers, New York.

Leighton, M.N.
1928 The Geological Aspects of Some of the Cahokia (Illinois) Mounds. *University of Illinois Bulletin.* Vol. 26 (No. 4), Pt. 2, pp. 109-143. Urbana.

Lewis, Henry von and George B. Douglas
1857 *Das Illustrirte Mississippithal.* Reprints of Rare Americana No. 3. Schmidt & Gunther, Leipzig, 1923.

Long, Stephen H.
1823 Account of an Expedition from Pittsburgh to The Rocky Mountains performed in the Years 1819, 1820. Compiled from the notes of Major Long, Mr. T. Say, and other gentlemen of

the party by Edwin James in *Early Western Travels 1748-1846,* Vol. 14, edited by Reuben Gold Thwaites. The Arthur H. Clark Company, 1905. Cleveland.

McAdams, Clark

1907   The Archaeology of Illinois. *Transactions of the Illinois State Historical Society for 1907,* pp. 35-47. Springfield.

McAdams, William

1881   Ancient Mounds of Illinois. *Proceedings of the American Association for the Advancement of Science. 29th Meeting held at Boston, Massachusetts, August, 1880,* pp. 710-718. Salem.

1882   Antiquities. In *History of Madison County, Illinois,* pp. 58-64. W. R. Brink & Co., Edwardsville, Illinois.

1883   *Antiquities of Cahokia or Monks Mound in Madison County, Illinois.* W. R. Brink, Edwardsville, Illinois.

1887   *Records of Ancient Races in the Mississippi Valley.* C. R. Barns Publishing Company, St. Louis.

1895   Archaeology. *Report of the Illinois Board of World's Fair Commissioners at the World's Columbian Exposition.* H. W. Rokker, Printer and Binder, Springfield.

McDermott, John Francis

1949   *Old Cahokia: A Narrative and Documents Illustrating the First Century of Its History.* Buechler Publishing Company, Belleville, Illinois.

Mason, Ronald J., and Gregory Perino

1961   Microblades at Cahokia, Illinois. *American Antiquity,* Vol. 26 (No. 4), pp. 553-557. Salt Lake City.

Meiners, Ray and Robert Grimm

1942   Uncovering an Ancient Village Site. *Hobbies—The Magazine for Collectors,* Vol. 47 (No. 7), pp. 99-100. Chicago.

Moorehead, Warren K.

1912   Archaeology of the Mississippi. *Transactions of the Illinois State Historical Society, for the Year 1910,* pp. 184-185. Publication No. 15 of the Illinois State Historical Library, Springfield.

1921   *Help Save the Cahokia Mounds.* Circular, August, 4 pages. Andover, Mass.

1922a   Preservation of the Cahokia Mounds. *The Wisconsin Archeologist,* (January), Vol. 1 (No. 1), (new series), pp. 25-27. Milwaukee.

1922b   The Cahokia Mounds: A Preliminary Report. *University of Illinois Bulletin,* Vol. 19 (No. 35), Urbana.

1923   The Cahokia Mounds: Part I, A Report of Progress by Warren
        K. Moorehead and Part I, A Report of Progress by Warren K.
        Moorehead and Part II, Some Geological Aspects by Morris M.
        Leighton. *University of Illinois Bulletin,* Vol. 21 (No. 6).
        Urbana.

1928   The Cahokia Mounds. *University of Illinois Bulletin,* Vol. 26 (No.
        4). Urbana.

Morrison, Anna R.

1914   Diary of a Journey from New York to Jacksonville (November
        11, 1840 to March 1, 1841). *Journal of the Illinois State
        Historical Society,* Vol. 7 (No. 1), pp. 34-51. Springfield.

Munson, Patrick J.

1966   *An Archaeological Survey of the "Wood River Terrace" and
        Adjacent Bottoms and Bluffs in Madison County, Illinois.*
        Illinois State Museum Preliminary Reports, No. 8. Springfield.

Obrecht, Rev. Father

1905   Letter to Clark McAdams regarding the Cahokia Mounds in
        "The Archaeology of Illinois" by Clark McAdams. In *Trans-
        actions of the Illinois State Historical Society for 1907,* pp.
        39-41. Springfield.

Oliver, William

1843   *Eight Months in Illinois; with Information to Emigrants.*
        William Andrew Mitchell, Newcastle upon Tyne. (Reprinted
        1924, by Walter M. Hill, The Torch Press, Cedar Rapids, Iowa.)

Orthwein, Walter E.

1965   Tests Show Monks Mound Not Wholly Man-Made. *St. Louis
        Globe-Democrat.* September 28, 1965, 3A. St. Louis.

Parmalee, Paul W.

1957   Vertebrate Remains from the Cahokia Site, Illinois. *Trans-
        actions of the Illinois State Academy of Science,* Vol. 50, pp.
        235-242. Springfield.

Parrish, Randall

1906   *Historic Illinois: The Romance of the Earlier Days,* 2nd
        edition. McClurg & Company, Chicago.

Peck, John Mason

1834   *Gazetteer of Illinois.* R. Goudy, Jacksonville.

1840   *The Travellers Directory for Illinois.* J. H. Colton, New York.

Peet, Stephen D.

1891a   The Cahokia Tablet. *The American Antiquarian,* Vol. 13 (No.
        1), pp. 58-59. Chicago.

1891b   The Great Cahokia Mound. *The American Antiquarian,* Vol. 13
        (No. 1), pp. 3-31. Chicago.

Perino, Gregory

1947 Cultural Problems at Cahokia. *Illinois State Archaeological Society Journal,* Vol. 4 (No. 3), pp. 14-17. Springfield.

1957 Cahokia. *Central States Archaeological Journal,* Vol. 3 (No. 3), pp. 84-88. Quincy, Illinois.

1959 Recent Information from Cahokia and Its Satellites *Central States Archaeological Journal,* Vol. 6 (No. 4), pp. 130-138. Quincy, Illinois.

Peterson, C. A.

1902 "The Mound Building Age in North America." Read Feb. 15, 1902 before Missouri State Historical Society. St. Louis.

Priest, Josiah

1833 *American Antiquities and Discoveries in the West,* 5th edition. Hoffman and White, Albany.

Putnam, F. W. and Dr. J. Patrick

1880 Twelfth Annual Report of the Peabody Museum. *Reports of the Peabody Museum of American Archaeology and Ethnology in Connection with Harvard University, 1876-79.* Vol. 2, Cambridge.

Ramey Family

1916 *The Mound Builders. The Greatest Monument of Prehistoric Man, Cahokia or Monks Mound.* 28 pages. Private Printing.

Randall, Emilius Oviatt

1908 *Masterpieces of Ohio Mound Builders.* Ohio State Archaeological and Historical Society. Columbus, Ohio.

Rau, Charles

1867 Indian Pottery. *Annual Report of the Smithsonian Institution, 1866,* pp. 346-355. Washington.

Reed, Nelson

1964 Cahokia. *The St. Louis Magazine: Bicentennial Issue,* February, Vol. 1 (No. 9), pp. 47ff. St. Louis.

Reed, Nelson A., John W. Bennett and James Warren Porter

1968 Solid Core Drilling of Monks Mound: Technique and Findings. *American Antiquity,* Vol. 33 (No. 2), pp. 137-148. Salt Lake City.

Reynolds, John

1879 *My Own Times: Embracing also the History of My Life.* Chicago Historical Society. Fergus Printing Company, Chicago.

Russell, John

1831 Western Antiquities. *Illinois Monthly Magazine,* March, 1831. Vandalia, Illinois.

Schoolcraft, Henry Rowe
  1825   *Travels in the Central Portions of the Mississippi Valley:*
          comprising observations on its mineral geography, internal
          resources, and aboriginal population. Collins and Hannay, New
          York.
Shetrone, Henry Clyde
  1930   *The Mound Builders.* D. Appleton and Company, New York.
Shipp, Barnard
  1897   *The Indian and Antiquities of America.* Sherman and
          Company, Philadelphia.
Short, John T.
  1880   *The North Americans of Antiquity.* Harper & Brothers, New
          York.
Silverberg, Robert
  1968   *Mound Builders of Ancient America: The Archaeology of a*
          Myth. New York Graphic Society Ltd., Greenwich, Con-
          necticut.
Smith, Harlan Ingersoll
  1902   The Great American Pyramid. *Harper's Monthly Magazine,* Vol.
          104, pp. 199-204. New York.
Smith, Harriet M.
  1942   Excavation of the Murdock Mound of the Cahokia Group.
          Journal of the Illinois State Archaeological Society, Vol. 1 (No.
          1), pp. 13-18. Springfield. (Mimeographed)
Snyder, John Francis
  1894   An Illinois "Teocalli." *The Archaeologist,* Vol. 2 (No. 9), pp.
          259-264. Waterloo, Indiana.
  1900   The Field for Archaeological Research in Illinois. *Transactions*
          of the Illinois State Historical Society for 1900, pp. 21-29.
          Springfield.
  1909   Prehistoric Illinois. Certain Indian Mounds Technically Con-
          sidered. *Journal of the Illinois State Historical Society,* Vols. 1
          and 2, pp. 31-40, 47-65, 71-92. Springfield.
  1911   Prehistoric Illinois. Its Psychozoic Problems. *Journal of the*
          Illinois State Historical Society, Vol. 4, pp. 288-302. Spring-
          field.
  1913   *The Prehistoric Mounds of Illinois.* Published by "The Monks
          of Cahokia," 1913. (pamphlet, p. 8)
  1914   Prehistoric Illinois—The Great Cahokia Mound. *Illinois State*
          Historical Society Journal, Vol. 6, pp. 506-508. Springfield.
  1917   The Great Cahokia Mound. *Illinois State Historical Society*
          Journal, Vol. 10, pp. 256-259. Springfield.

Squier, E. G. and E. H. Davis
    1848   Ancient Monuments of the Mississippi Valley: Comprising the Results of Extensive Original Surveys and Explorations. *Smithsonian Contributions to Knowledge,* Vol. 1, p. 174. Washington.

Sutter, J. R.
    1891   Inscription with Date of 1676 Near St. Louis. *American Antiquarian,* Vol. 13, pp. 350-351. Chicago.

Thomas, Cyrus
    1894   Report on the Mound Explorations of the Bureau of Ethnology. *12th Annual Report of the Bureau of Ethnology, 1890-91,* pp. 131-134. Washington.
    1907   Cahokia or Monks Mound. *American Anthropologist* (new series), Vol. 9, pp. 362-365. Menasha.

Throop, Addison J.
    1928   *The Mound Builders of Illinois.* Call Printing Company. East St. Louis, Illinois.

Titterington, P. F.
    1933   The Cahokia Mound Group and Its Surface Material. *Wisconsin Archeologist,* Vol. 13 (No. 1), pp. 7-14. Milwaukee.
    1938   *The Cahokia Mound Group and Its Village Site Materials.* St. Louis, Missouri.

Townley, E. C.
    1927   Some Mound Builders in Illinois. *Art and Archaeology,* Vol. 24 (No. 6), pp. 234-238. Washington.

Tucker, Sara Jones (compiled by)
    1942   *Indian Villages of the Illinois County, Vol. II, Scientific Paper, Illinois State Museum. Part I, Atlas.* State of Illinois, Springfield, Ill.

Udden, J. A. and E. W. Shaw
    1915   *Geologic Atlas of the United States: Belleville-Breese Folio No. 195 Illinois.* U. S. Geological Survey. Washington.

Vogel, Joseph O.
    1964   *A Preliminary Report on the Analysis of Ceramics from the Cahokia Area at the Illinois State Museum.* University Microfilms, Inc. Ann Arbor, Michigan.

Walton, Clyde C. (editor)
    1962   *John Francis Snyder: Selected Writings.* The Illinois State Historical Society. Springfield.

Whitlock, W. H.
    1933   Who Built Monks Mound? *Illinois State Historical Society Journal,* Vol. 26, pp. 151-161. Springfield.

Wild, J. C.
    1841   *The Valley of the Mississippi; Illustrated in a Series of Views.*
           Chambers and Knapp, St. Louis.
Williams, Stephen and John M. Goggin
    1956   The Long-nosed God Mask in Eastern United States. *The*
           Missouri Archaeologist, Vol. 18 (No. 3), pp. 1-72. Columbia,
           Mo.
Wittry, Warren L.
    1964   An American Woodhenge. *Cranbrook Institute of Science News*
           Letter, Vol. 33 (No. 9), pp. 102-107. Bloomfield Hills,
           Michigan.

Publications of the Illinois Archaeological Survey—

BULLETIN SERIES

Illinois Archaeology (Bulletin 1)

An authoritative summary of the prehistory and early history of the state of Illinois, written by six archaeologists. Illustrated with seven drawings and two maps. Price $1.00.

Indian Mounds and Villages in Illinois (Bulletin 2)   Out of Print

Chicago Area Archaeology (Bulletin 3)   Out of Print

Reports on Illinois Prehistory: 1 (Bulletin 4)   Out of Print

Middle Woodland Sites in Illinois (Bulletin 5)   Out of Print

Hopewell and Woodland Site Archaeology in Illinois (Bulletin 6)   Out of Print

Exploration into Cahokia Archaeology, edited by M. L. Fowler
Rev. edition (Bulletin 7)

Six contributions from participants to a symposium on Cahokia held in 1968 and others, as well as a preface by the editor and a bibliography of archaeology of Cahokia. Illustrated with 73 maps, photographs, and drawings, Price $3.00.

Mississippian Site Archaeology in Illinois I: Site Reports from the St. Louis and Chicago Areas (Bulletin 8)

Four site reports record different aspects of Illinois prehistory during the Mississippian period. Aspects of burial practices in the region of the great Cahokia site are documented in reports on the Schild Cemetery (Greene Co.), the Krueger Cemetery (Monroe Co.), and the Yokem Mounds (Pike Co.). Excavations of an Upper Mississippian village are described in a report on the Knoll Spring Site (Cook Co.). Illustrated with 110 photographs, figures, and maps; 264 pages. Price $4.00.

Late Woodland Site Archaeology in Illinois I: Investigations in South-central Illinois (Bulletin 9)

Reports of archaeological investigations at nine Late Woodland sites in three regions. Both village and burial sites of the Late Woodland period are described from the Lower Illinois valley, the middle Kanskaskia valley, and the American Bottom area of the Mississippi valley, Illustrated with 110 photographs, figures and maps; 232 pages. Price $3.75.